D0065908

FAD-FREE

FREE

MANAGEMENT

FAD-FREE

MANAGEMENT

THE SIX PRINCIPLES

THAT DRIVE

SUCCESSFUL COMPANIES

AND THEIR LEADERS

RICHARD G. HAMERMESH

KNOWLEDGEXCHANGE

Santa Monica

Knowledge Exchange, LLC
1299 Ocean Avenue
Santa Monica, California 90401
In Association with Wordworks, Inc.,
Boston, Massachusetts

Jacket design by Russell Gordon
Text design by Mark Heliger

1 2 3 4 5 6 7 8 9-VA-99 98 97 96
First printing October 1996
ISBN: 1-888232-20-X

Knowledge Exchange books are available at special discounts for bulk
purchases by corporations, institutions, and other organizations.
For more information, please contact Knowledge Exchange, LLC, at:
(310) 394-5995 (voice line) or kex@kex.com (e-mail).

■

For Lorie, who is everything

Contents

■

Acknowledgments

B ecause this book draws on all three areas of my professional life, as well as the personal support I have
received, I have more than a few people to acknowledge.

From my academic past, I would like to acknowledge the
immense impact the following individuals have had on me:
Kenneth Andrews, Raymond Bauer, Joseph Bower, Alfred
Chandler, and Jay Lorsch. They taught me both intellectual
rigor and an academic's healthy skepticism.

From my executive education and consulting side, I
want to acknowledge my deepest appreciation to my fellow
founding partners of the Center for Executive Development
(CED)—Doug Anderson and John Cady—as well as to my
two more recent partners—Todd Jick and Frank Cespedes.
Together we have not only created a successful business
but, more importantly, have figured out how to use executive education to substantially change the direction of
corporations. Our experiences together have provided
fertile ground for the ideas in this book.

From my management and investment side, I owe the

deepest gratitude to my partners in the businesses we have purchased, managed, and grown. In particular, I want to acknowledge Amin Khoury, Paul Marshall, Joe O'Donnell, and Hansjoerg Wyss. As experienced executives, they have made me acutely aware of the realities of business life and of the need for actionable ideas, not complicated theories.

As I turned to the actual writing of the manuscript, my 11-year absence from the world of writing and publishing was made immeasurably easier by the support I received from my literary agent, Helen Rees, and Donna Carpenter of Wordworks, Inc. They believed in the ideas of this book from the beginning, and its completion and publication are a credit to them. From Wordworks, I would also like to acknowledge the fine work of Mark Fischetti and Mel Pine, as well as the very special support I received from Martha Lawler and G. Patton Wright. The people at my publisher, Knowledge Exchange, also deserve recognition. In particular I want to acknowledge Lorraine Spurge for her commitment, enthusiasm, and constant encouragement for the ideas put forth in the book.

Finally, this book would not have happened without the immense personal support of my wife, Lorie. Ever since I mentioned the idea for this book in the summer of 1993, Lorie has encouraged, prodded, and supported me in this effort. An accomplished painter, Lorie knows the trials and tribulations of originality and creativity. She has taught me so much while providing the safety that is inherent in reciprocal love.

■

Preface

It's Easy Enough for Me to Say

I will make this short if not sweet.

The principles of good management are not complicated, nor do they change over time. My job—describing good management—is easy. Your job—managing—is difficult. I therefore pledge to keep this book simple.

I've been brooding over the ideas in this book for more than two decades as an academic, a management consultant, and an entrepreneur. It all started back in 1974 when I took an oral exam to qualify for a doctorate in business policy at Harvard Business School. I had already taken the written exam, churning out page after page of my understanding of obscure theories and intricate strategies. Now I was talking about more of the same, and the more I talked, the better I felt. I was passing the exam; I just knew it. All that remained between me and my doctorate was my thesis. But then one of the school's graybeards threw me a question I wasn't prepared to answer.

"I can tell by your essays that you have mastered the management literature," he said. "But tell me, is there anything in all these books you have read about management and leadership that wasn't already known by Moses?"

In the long silence that followed, I tried to remember what I could about Moses. Then I ventured, "Probably not."

I reasoned that Moses knew a lot about what we call organizational change. Why else would he lead the Israelites for 40 years on a journey that could be walked in four days? Clearly, he needed time to change his people's culture from one of passivity and slavery to one of self-government. He needed time, also, to implement one of the world's earliest value statements—the Ten Commandments. And he needed time to shape his people into fast-reacting self-starters who could be depended on in battle. Only then could they be worthy of a land of milk and honey.

I passed the test, received my doctorate, and took a faculty position at Harvard Business School. I hope I asked my students questions as enlightening as the one that professor asked me.

In 1986, I left academe to cofound with three Harvard colleagues the Center for Executive Development (CED), an executive education and consulting firm in Cambridge, Massachusetts, devoted to advising and educating executives. As CED's managing partner, I have advised more than 100 companies. I have also taken an ownership position and management role in five other businesses in industries ranging from aircraft seats and interiors to medical devices to extruded polypropylene films. I have also served on the boards of two public companies, Applied Extension Technologies and BE Aerospace. Increasingly, my clients—including such giants as AT&T Corporation, Chrysler Corporation, Eli Lilly and Company, General Electric Company, Johnson & Johnson, Price Waterhouse LLP, and R. R. Donnelley & Sons Company—have asked me to educate their people about what managers really need to know. I hope I have nudged them away from fads and back to the basics—to what Moses knew.

The fundamentals don't change. They really don't. To neglect them while chasing after the latest mass-marketed wisdom is not only to pass up the best road to success, but also to alienate the workforce. There is no quicker way to make businesspeople cynical than to shower them with one fashionable buzzword after another—*continuous improvement, high-performance organization, key performance indicators, open book, open door, management by objective, quality circles, zero-based budgeting,* and so on. You know a trend has gone too far when it is the subject of jokes on the comic page of your daily newspaper. Well, check out *Dilbert,* the strip by Scott Adams, which elevates cynicism about faddish management to an art form.

After I moved from academia to my office at CED, I decided to start chucking out every book I had not looked at in the last two years. At Harvard, I had close to 50 linear feet of books on my shelves. At CED, I have whittled the collection down to four feet.

Four feet of books, I grant you, contain a good many more words than the Ten Commandments. So does this book, but then I'm not Moses, and my six principles aren't going to give direction to Western civilization for the next 3,000 years. They are like the Ten Commandments in one respect, however: They are as simple to understand as they are difficult to carry out. In the pages that follow I will explain them. You will have to carry them out.

Dilbert® by Scott Adams

Dilbert reprinted by permission of United Feature Syndicate, Inc.

■

Introduction

Bumper-Car Management

O ne of the most popular spots in any carnival or amusement park is the bumper car ride. Children wait
patiently, clutching their tickets. When their turn comes, they
run expectantly throughout the enclosure in search of the best
vehicle—the fastest, heaviest, most maneuverable. Then they
strap themselves in and, at the sound of a bell, find themselves able to drive for a few minutes.

Their joy is inexpressible. At an age when they can control
so little, they now control a car, albeit a tiny one, all by themselves. Off they go, deftly dodging and slamming as many
other cars as possible. The ride stops when the bell rings
again, but many of the children get back in line, eager once
again to find that best car.

But, of course, there is no such car.

When I see corporations going from management fad to
management fad, I think about those children and their
bumper cars. It's as though businesspeople feel just as power-
less as eight-year-olds and dash from management by
objective to continuous improvement to whichever trend next

1

catches their fancy and brings them the illusion of controlling their destiny.

And, you know what? No matter which vehicle they hop into, they still get bumped around.

But it isn't an amusement park that these grown-ups are playing in, and their vehicles do not have spring-mounted bumpers to absorb the shocks. In fact, the result of all this management fad hopping is a frantic leadership, a dispirited workforce, and a dead-end company.

One place where this happened was Digital Equipment Corporation. Digital was a notable growth company of the 1970s and 1980s, riding the success of its minicomputers and networking. Over the three years beginning in 1987, Digital earned a total of more than $3.5 billion in profits. A 1988 *Business Week* cover story called the company "a potent No. 2 to industry leader International Business Machines Corporation."

In 1990, Digital suffered its first quarterly loss. In the four years that followed, the company hemorrhaged more than $5.3 billion.

What went wrong? As Digital became increasingly successful in the 1980s, its managers never saw a fad or a hot new idea they didn't like. They not only went from bumper car to bumper car but, even worse, tried to ride all of them at once. The message that the workers heard went something like this: "Please develop a vision and be empowered and take a risk—and work in teams while you're doing it. And don't forget to manage by objective. And please get on with the quality movement. Oh, and by the way, manage with the fifth discipline and get close to your customers."

Wildly confusing directives like those can turn a bright, vigorous, enthusiastic workforce into a pack of near-zombies. When Digital told people both to be autonomous, take risks, and work in teams, for example, it put them in a hard-to-win situation. Individual risk-taking calls for decisiveness and experimentation, whereas teamwork calls for due process and inclusive participation. Either might be appropriate at a given time, but emphasizing both at once is asking for trouble. People may go along as best they can, but when asked to do the impossible, they shut down. If the bosses are having so much fun hopping bumper cars, it's not a good idea to tell them that they are going nowhere.

At Digital, working in teams was not enough. The teams had to be self-managed. That tends to slow decision-making to a crawl—and Digital competes in the computer industry, where a new generation of technology appears every 18 months. The company's managers were much more interested in *how* things got done than in *what* was being done.

When I was called in as a consultant in the late 1980s, like all outsiders, I was first treated to a grilling on the latest fads and buzzwords. Instead of asking what I could do to help with the company's problems, my clients at Digital wanted to know if I understood terms like *managing with the fifth discipline*. That I passed their test is no great source of pride to me.

Even though management played the bumper-car game, profits still grew. It wasn't until some time after the company made a series of blunders that its underlying difficulties became manifest. Perhaps the biggest of these errors was the $1 billion the company spent in an attempt to enter the mainframe computer market. As I gave talks at Digital, I learned that many midlevel executives believed it was a terrible mistake to invest that much money in an effort to attack IBM at its strongest point. They believed the $1 billion could be better spent developing personal computers, the high-growth product.

They were right but unable to raise their objections. With managers preoccupied with chasing fads, they determined it was hopeless to try to disagree about anything.

Digital's record year was 1988, when it made $1.3 billion. Even then, Digital's costs were out of line with those of its key competitors. Some of its financial indicators—for example, return on capital—were dismal. Managers, however, were busy congratulating themselves on the high profits and soaring stock price—and its enlightened (though decidedly varied) approach to running a company.

In 1989 and 1990, as corporate results headed south, Digital held endless meetings, but no one would face the real problems: wasted resources and the inability to control costs. Finally, after a change of management in 1992, Digital stopped chasing fads and started seeing reality. The new CEO, Robert Palmer, reorganized the company around its product lines, sold off noncore assets, and slashed costs. A much smaller Digital returned to profitability in 1995, but whether the new managers can achieve long-term prosperity is still an open question. Let's hope they have the will to stay away from bumper cars.

Why did Digital rush to so many fads? The same reason other companies do so: It's a tough and confusing business world out there—and getting more so every day. Running a business has never been easy, and in the last quarter century it has become tougher than ever. Businesspeople face fierce competition at home and abroad. Because governments around the world—including that of the U.S.—have liberalized their economies, businesspeople now have unprecedented opportunities. But to succeed, they need to master rapidly changing technology, cope with more price- and quality-conscious customers, and make their way through market environments that look less and less like a checkerboard and more and more like an open playing field.

Companies that performed, say, at the B-minus level might have been able to get by in the 1950s and 1960s, but not anymore. The frustration to do better helps fuel the search for something new, for the easy answer. Hence, the rush to the current fad. Once the latest "management by" becomes popular, its adherents recommend it to their friends, and *Business Week* puts it on the cover, and you're no longer a good manager unless you are using it, too.

Companies grope for whatever they believe will give them an edge. Often at their peril, they stretch for that brass ring. Dozens of business books roll off the presses each month, each offering a strategy for grasping the ring without losing balance and direction.

Each time a company's employees are called on to master yet another gimmick, their alienation grows. Because employment anxiety is high, they go along to get along. Jerry Harvey, professor of Management Science at George Washington University, calls this sort of passivity the Abilene Paradox. He came up with the term when he was visiting his in-laws in west Texas. One hot Sunday night, his father-in-law suggested that the family have dinner at a diner in Abilene—a drive of more than 50 miles. Everyone deferentially piled into the car for a miserable ride and a wretched dinner. Back at the in-laws' house later, someone asked: "Who's idea was that anyway?" Nobody wanted to accuse Dad of botching the evening, so no one answered the question. The irony was that Dad never particularly wanted to drive to Abilene in the first place. He just tossed out the idea because he thought the family was getting bored. In an effort to be accommodating, everyone in the family had suffered through a dismal drive and an indigestible dinner.

I often tell that story during the management courses I run for my clients. I ask for examples of the Abilene Paradox in their companies. We discuss how they happened, what to do about them, and how to avoid this type of madness in the future.

Here's a sampling of people's responses.

- "We're all running around setting up quality circles that don't do us a bit of good."

- "We've been told we're supposed to manage by walking around, and it seems stupid and shallow to us."

- "We spend incredible resources trying to win quality and management awards when we need to focus better on our fundamentals."

No one, sad to say, had spoken up to the powers that be or even gone so far as to say, "There's a kernel of usefulness in this program, but we need to modify it for our company."

Often when I ask people in these groups whether their company has a vision statement, they say, "Sure," but they don't have the slightest notion of what it is. At one company I visited no one even knew where to find a copy of the statement. As far as they were concerned, *anything* that came down from on high could be dismissed in advance as a tedious and useless new management technique.

Even the best-managed companies aren't immune to the condition of passive-followerhood now and then.

I admire Johnson & Johnson and have done a lot of work with its top 500 managers. When I did the Abilene exercise with them, many complained about having to spend time at an institute promoted by a consulting company Johnson & Johnson had hired to train them to improve quality. Although the company spent millions of dollars on that program, it just didn't fit Johnson & Johnson's needs. What's worse, the managers felt proselytized, not trained.

Our seminars got the problem out on the table, and

Johnson & Johnson developed its own way to put the quality movement into place. At a company as large and diversified as Johnson & Johnson, each division may need its own approach to quality. Our seminars helped open a channel of communication that had been blocked, and that was enough to get a start on a solution.

Johnson & Johnson is an exception, however. Too many companies are looking for quick fixes. In their 1982 bestseller *In Search of Excellence*, Tom Peters and Robert Waterman emphasized the importance of a strong corporate culture. I was still on the faculty at Harvard Business School at the time, and I got a call from the Human Resources vice president of a Fortune 50 company who had just read the book.

"I've heard good things about you," he said, "and I need your help."

"What's the problem you need help with?" I asked.

"We'd like a corporate culture."

I was tempted to say: "Oh, that will be no problem. Let me open up my desk drawer here and pull out three or four. We'll see which one you'd like."

The notion that a productive corporate culture could be had by merely calling in an outsider captures the absurdity of this desire for a quick fix. Running a successful business is hard work, and nobody needs to be distracted by fads from getting on with the simple yet difficult task of managing well.

What are the basics? I've identified six principles of good management. They're easy to express but hard to put into practice—so hard that I doubt there's a company anywhere that embodies all of them. Even the best companies I know successfully embody only a few of these principles, but what sets them apart from the rest is that they know where they are weak and they strive to do better.

In brief, here are the six principles.

Principle One: Get Real

Winning companies see the environment for what it is and themselves for what they are. It is all too easy to perceive things as we wish them to be, not as they are.

Like everyone else, businesspeople are prone to overestimate their own strengths and their competitors' weaknesses. Many people harbor the illusion that they and their family, ethnic group, religion, country, or neighborhood are superior to all others. Within limits, this is what social scientists call healthy narcissism. And it can be a good thing: After all, we cannot live without a sense of a solid foundation and self-esteem. But the business world is different: When we believe that *our company* is superior to all others in its market, we are asking for failure.

This wasn't always the case. Joseph Schumpeter's famous remark that capitalism engages in a process of "creative destruction" is liberally bandied about these days. General Motors, Sears, and IBM, however, were not destroyed, creatively or otherwise. Quite the opposite; they did the destroying. Even today, they can still say—with some degree of truth—that their companies are superior to all others.

The difference is that in the current business world, it's a trivial truth, frighteningly contingent on all sorts of factors over which those "superior" companies have little or no control. They do their best to exert control, of course. You could build an entire library around the books written on strategic planning alone. But you could burn it to the ground for all the good it will do if you are not basing your thinking on the real world.

Early in my career, I didn't get it. I didn't believe anyone could run a business successfully—with large amounts of (other people's) money and many jobs at stake—without looking squarely at reality. Now I realize that the view may be too scary for many managers, and that it's the exceptional person who sees his or her company and business environment clearly. I tell my clients to go to the movies when they want fantasies. On the job, they need to work hard to build a reality-based culture, and the only way they can achieve it is to seek out the truth both inside and outside their organizations.

Principle Two: Get Moving

Once you have a grip on reality, you need to act on it. You may be a great observer of trends, but it won't do you a shred of good if you don't act on what you know.

What seems so obvious is often overlooked. Consider the frustration of middle-level and junior managers who see opportunities but cannot get an okay from senior management to exploit them. My seminars over the years have been filled by these people.

Maybe *action* is not a problem in some small entrepreneurial companies that have not yet had time to develop much of a structure. But sooner or later, in companies of any size, risk aversion sets in. Going to meetings and merely studying a situation take priority over doing something about it. People are afraid to be wrong, so they pursue the perfect answer before committing to action. Since perfection is impossible, nothing gets done.

It's fiendishly difficult to create a climate where it's healthy to be wrong once in a while.

Principle Three: Speak the Truth

This, too, is far more difficult than it sounds. Speaking the truth is quite different from not telling lies, which is usually quite easy. Speaking the truth requires candor, frankness, straightforwardness, openness—in other words, positive, proactive honesty—as well as intelligence, courage, imagination, self-respect, and a sense of belonging. These qualities are not in great supply in many companies—not at least in the combination required for corporate success. If they were, bosses wouldn't shirk from telling employees how to improve, and workers would speak up when management makes a mistake.

Many top-level managers I know can breeze through presentations to securities analysts or shareholders, but they break into a sweat at the prospect of a one-on-one conversation with a subordinate about a performance issue.

All communication needs to be open and honest—from bosses, from employees, and especially from the company about how the business is doing. In some companies, managers hoard information to gain what they think will be an advantage over their peers, but a much more common block to honest communication is the desire to be accommodating.

Indeed, managers who think they are being nice by waffling on performance reviews aren't showing much respect for their employees, who can improve only if they have all the information, including the bad news. Likewise, workers who hold back when they think the company is going in the wrong direction can't have much trust in the company, or in its ability to recognize its mistakes and correct them.

Building a winning organization requires developing a climate in which solidarity and mutual respect generate trust, and trust generates courage and fresh thinking, and "all of the above" generate honesty. This is not like rolling off a log.

Principle Four: Inspire Concretely

Yes, I know that vision statements have been fashionable in recent years and that most are nothing more than platitudes. That doesn't change the fact that companies need vision, and vision has been around since humans first organized into groups.

It doesn't matter what you call it, but a winning vision has three components:

◆ VALUES
What does the company stand for? What are the principles and beliefs that guide our behavior?

◆ PURPOSE
Why are we working here? What do we accomplish that's useful in the world?

◆ MISSION
What are we trying to achieve? What are our most important goals?

To be fully effective, companies need all three elements of vision, and they need to translate the abstract elements of the vision into concrete terms. The values guide the workers' work. The (larger) purpose gives them a sense of meaning, of having a useful place in the scheme of things. The mission provides an objective, or series of objectives, by which they can measure their progress and performance. Merely posting such a mission on a bulletin board for all to see, however, is not enough. Through concrete actions and rewards, you must inspire employees to incorporate the mission statement, to live it in everything they do for the organization.

At first, many will be cynical about these objectives. The clouds of cynicism about vision statements arise because of two factors. First, these visions tend to be incomplete. Most often they present some lofty and vague values such as the "pursuit of excellence" without tying the statement to what people do in the real world. Second—and the more serious problem—they don't reflect the company's reality in concrete terms. Empty talk about "valuing our people" is not going to move anyone in an organization that treats its employees or customers with indifference or contempt.

Identifying the company's values, purpose, and mission can be a constructive exercise, especially if the results are printed and distributed as a vision statement. Whatever the statement is called or however it looks, what's important is that the elements of vision are openly discussed, debated, incorporated, and *reflected in people's behavior from top to bottom*. Only then can everyone in the organization own shared values, purpose, and mission.

Principle Five: Challenge False Paradoxes

At the best companies, people aren't tyrannized by trade-offs. They learn to shed "either/or" thinking. In Western cultures we tend to see problems as dualisms calling for a choice of one over the other. Some of the most creative thinkers, however, have learned how to avoid that trap. They have learned the power of "both/and" thinking.

Is there really a conflict, for example, between short-term and long-term performance? Many analysts will tell you that there is. But in reality you've got to perform today, or you won't be around tomorrow. And you'd better lay the groundwork for tomorrow while you are at it today. That's what management is all about.

Similarly, you've got to meet your customers' expectations and make a profit. It took the Japanese to show us it's possible to produce high-quality products at low cost. American managers had been willing to accept a trade-off between quality and cost.

Once you get used to "both/and" thinking, you'll see more and more opportunities to use it. Winning companies refuse to choose between a fast decision and a good one. They design a decision-making process that surfaces just the right amount of information needed for a quick decision—helping them achieve Principle Two, Get Moving.

Principle Six: Lead

Successful companies have strong leaders not just at the top but throughout the organization. Good leadership may be hard to accomplish, but it's a lot easier to find good leaders than it is to find a good theory of leadership.

Give me a day in a company to talk with various managers, and I can usually tell whether the company is well led. If I get a consistent and enthusiastic answer when I ask about the company's goals, I know I'm in the right place. If the answers aren't consistent, the company isn't well led. If all I hear is "What goal?" then leadership is absent altogether.

That's why I'm amazed with the absence of leadership in so many companies, given how much has been written about the quality. With so many confusing theories in the air, people slip into forgetting the basics: Leadership is the ability to set clear direction, to develop the trust of your people, and to produce winning results.

You can lead by involving workers in the decision making or by decree, but you've got to lead. Trust grows out of the other principles, especially *Speak the Truth*. When a manager is clear about exactly what the organization faces, that forthrightness inspires trust. And as for winning, it's the most overlooked element of leadership.

■ ■ ■ ■ ■

I've been asked what a company would look like if it could live up to all six of these principles. When I think of an answer, I start to hear former Beatle John Lennon's song "Imagine" running through my mind. For some people, a winning, fad-free company may be as idealistic as the world Lennon imagined, but I think it's a reasonable and attainable goal.

When I imagine a company that lives by all six of the principles, I see a company where people:

◆ Get real

◆ Get moving

◆ Speak the truth

◆ Inspire concretely

◆ Challenge false paradoxes

◆ Lead

Get Real

- ◆ Reward each other for getting problems out in the open early rather than hiding them.

- ◆ Promptly acknowledge their mistakes.

- ◆ Pay relentless attention to whether they're keeping up with trends in their industry, with technology, and with what their competitors are doing.

- ◆ Seek out the views of insiders and outsiders about the organization's performance.

- ◆ Never become self-satisfied.

Get Moving

- ◆ Analyze problems only to the extent needed to yield insights and then take action on those insights.

- ◆ Understand that the risk of doing nothing is often greater than the risk of making a change.

- ◆ Emphasize fixing problems over fixing blame for creating them.

- ◆ Organize meetings so that each has a stated purpose, a written agenda, and an announced specific length.

Speak the Truth

- ◆ Accept with eagerness and without threat any criticism of themselves, each other, and the company's performance.

- ◆ Discuss business results openly, without sugarcoating, throughout the organization.

- ◆ Communicate without obfuscation.

- ◆ Tell each other how they are doing and where they stand, even if the news is bad.

- ◆ Air gripes and criticisms openly, not behind each other's backs.

- ◆ Understand how to be direct and candid without being mean.

- ◆ Admit it when they don't know the answer to a question.

Inspire Concretely

◆ Draw inspiration from the company's vision, which gives everyone a sense of unity.

◆ Understand what the vision statement means in their day-to-day business lives.

◆ Challenge and modify the vision statement over time as a living document.

◆ Believe their work is important and useful.

◆ Feel the collective thrill that comes with trying to achieve a common challenging goal.

Challenge False Paradoxes

◆ Accept tough trade-offs as part of life and recognize that this is what managers are being paid to do.

◆ Think first, when faced with a dilemma, about how to win it all, not about what to sacrifice.

Lead

◆ Speak with a consistent voice about the organization's goals and problems.

◆ Assure that the major purposes and objectives are widely understood throughout the organization.

◆ Trust their leaders, not because the leaders are nice or charismatic, but because they tell the truth.

◆ Share the responsibility to lead when called upon.

This winning company produces results. Management places no premium on talk or appearances; it rewards merit. Winning people get ahead; shallow self-promoters do not.

This company not only benchmarks other companies but finds itself benchmarked as a model of best practices. And, of course, this company's products and services are winners; they are superior.

John Lennon acknowledges that people would think him a dreamer. Every idealist feels the cynicism as if it were sandpaper against the skin. None of this is easy. It's a lot to ask of any workforce, but it's a goal—a stretch goal, one that pushes us beyond what we think our limits are.

In the chapters that follow, I'll discuss each of the six principles in turn and offer suggestions on how to put them to work in your organization.

Principle One

GET REAL

How to put truth on the table, acknowledge mistakes, surface problems, and generally see yourself and your industry clearly.

How you can gain if you do.

How you will lose if you don't.

As part of a seminar I led in 1982, I asked a group of General Motors Corporation marketing executives how their company was doing. The answer was: "Fine, thanks." They said GM's market share was either flat or rising in recent years.

That didn't seem possible to me. At the time, I noticed fewer and fewer GM cars in parking lots and on highways. So

I asked these executives how they measured market share.

It couldn't be simpler, they explained. Just take the number of cars GM makes in a year and divide by the total of all cars produced in North America. By that arithmetic, GM's 1982 market share was 42 percent and holding steady.

Managing GM with those numbers, those executives might as well have been driving with blinders over their eyes. Their definition of market share ignored imports. All the Japanese and German imports that were rapidly filling up U.S. streets, simply didn't count. When I raised that issue, the participants insisted that the relevant universe—what they really had to worry about—was the cars produced in North America.

What they should have worried about was imports, which accounted for almost 25 percent of the American market in 1982. That influx occurred as a result of the steep climb in gasoline prices that followed the oil embargoes of the 1970's and the imports' high quality and low cost. If GM had been measuring its market share in terms of all cars *sold* in North America, it would have seen its market share fall from about 45 percent in 1973 to 35 percent in 1982: a far cry from the 42 percent share its executives claimed.

$10 Billion Worth of Reality

GM wasn't ignoring the imports altogether. In 1979, it had introduced a line of front-wheel-drive compacts to compete with Hondas, Toyotas, Volkswagens, and other imports. But a new product line wasn't nearly enough. To defeat—not merely to compete with—the imports, GM had to recognize that it was in a crisis calling for strong actions to reduce costs and improve quality. More than a decade later, GM President and CEO John F. Smith put it this way: "What we needed to do—and we were late getting going on it—was fix our core business."

The company's failure did indeed matter. At the time of

my seminar, the company was already nine years into what would become a 20-year trend.

In 1982, the GM executives couldn't see the future, but if they had looked at the present without distortion, they would have realized that they had already lost 10 percentage points of market share. This fact might have served as a wake-up call to take immediate action or risk losing the battle. Indeed, it would have been better for them if they had done so a decade earlier. By 1976, they should have recognized the seriousness of the threat. Instead, here they were in 1982, still thinking their business was doing "fine, thanks."

GM's failure to see reality and act appropriately laid the foundation for the devastation the company suffered in the early 1990s, when it lost close to $10 billion in three years (1990–92). A year of chaos and a series of boardroom upheavals led to the ouster of Robert Stempel as CEO in 1992, the third in a line of chief executive officers who, since 1973, had failed to act decisively enough.

This time, though, management finally realized the fix it was in. The board appointed John F. (Jack) Smith, Jr., who now had to cope with permanently lower volumes and market share. His only options were to slash costs, reorganize drastically, and downsize severely. By 1996, he had announced thousands of layoffs, close to 15 percent of the workforce, with more to come. In the 1990s GM continues to pay heavily for the oversights of the 1970s and 1980s, and any real rebuilding of the company must await completion of the downsizing. For those who wear blinders for long enough, learning to see without them is a long and painful process. Time will tell whether GM can recover full use of its eyes.

It's Easy to See the Other Guy's Reality

What took the world's largest industrial company so long to see reality? Was it just a massive case of the dumbs? It is so easy to feel superior. But GM has lots of company: We all tend to see things the way we want them to be. When I tell the GM story at seminars, people respond at first with a joke or an assertion of their superiority. Then, as people give this example more thought, I see the pain of recognition spread over their faces. Soon someone says, "Hey, who are we kidding? In our company we do the same thing."

You don't have to look further than the financial services industry to find an almost identical case. Full-service brokerage houses like to measure their market share against that of other full-service brokers—Merrill Lynch, Dean Witter, and Smith Barney, for example. That measure, however, ignores the business these companies have lost to discounters such as Charles Schwab and Fidelity Brokerage. Seeing reality seems like a snap as long as we are looking at another company or another industry. It's seeing our own reality that is so difficult.

Eight Things to Get Real About

I've identified eight realities that companies most often misperceive. It's a useful list to examine periodically.

1 YOUR STRENGTH IN YOUR MARKET
This is the one that GM and the full-service brokerage houses have trouble with. They miscalculate their market share. In some industries, the numbers representing market share aren't easy to come by. This makes it all the easier to avoid the issue. Don't.

2 YOUR QUALITY, ESPECIALLY AS COMPARED WITH YOUR COMPETITORS'
Companies have a tendency to overestimate their own quality and minimize the advantage a competitor's

products and services have. Ask an executive of one of the major oil companies about its gasolines and lubricants, and you will hear about their quality edge even though you are talking about standardized commodities. The trouble is that the person you are talking to really believes what he or she is saying.

---

3 WHAT YOUR CUSTOMERS THINK OF YOU

Everyone wants to be loved. Companies are quick to believe their customers love them and enjoy doing business with them. They are slow to recognize reservations that customers have about dealing with them and to hear their complaints about products and services. IBM enjoyed loyalty from its big commercial customers for many years but misjudged how far these clients could be pushed. When the time came for these "loyal" customers to buy a personal computer for practically every office, many of them bought the cheaper IBM clones.

---

4 WHY YOUR NONCUSTOMERS AREN'T DOING BUSINESS WITH YOU

In all likelihood, it's not because they are stupid and foolish. To discover why they are not buying your products, you need to talk to them. Ironically, most companies spend a lot more time and money surveying those customers they have than those who shop elsewhere. It should be the other way around. Apple Computer, for example, has wallowed so long in the enthusiastic support of its customers that it has ignored the much larger market of computer users with incompatible machines. Talking about Apple's self-absorption, Steve Jobs, its founder and former chairman, said: "It's amazing how different reality looks when you are inside Apple."

5 **THE POTENCY OF YOUR COMPETITORS**
The most common example of this insider-distortion is underestimating the strength of what seem like small, niche competitors. Sears, which enjoyed a position as the store of America's heartland, didn't see the threat from Kmart and Wal-Mart until these discounters began leading the fierce competition. Well into the 1980s, Sears reportedly didn't even mention Wal-Mart in strategy positioning papers.

6 **THE COST POSITION OF YOUR COMPETITORS, ESPECIALLY AS COMPARED WITH YOUR OWN**
It's hard to believe your competitor keeps costs lower than yours. Caterpillar Inc. had this problem in the 1980s when Komatsu increasingly invaded Caterpillar's market with lower-priced earth-moving equipment. In 1981 Caterpillar's chairman and CEO, Lee L. Morgan, was quoted as saying that he wasn't concerned about Komatsu's lower prices because the quality of the Japanese company's products was proportionately lower. He was wrong. Komatsu simply knew how to manufacture for less. Caterpillar was doing 80 percent of its manufacturing in the United States, much of it in unionized plants. Over the next few years, Komatsu captured 10 percentage points of Caterpillar's market share.

7 THE POTENTIAL IMPACT OF EMERGING TECHNOLOGIES OR MARKET SEGMENTS

When you get comfortable and start feeling secure, that's when to step up vigilance. Here again, IBM provides the example of what not to do. In 1974, it invented a microprocessor called RISC, which could simplify and speed up computing, but it underestimated RISC's market potential and failed to pursue the technology. That left the field wide open for its competition. Both Digital Equipment Corporation and IBM downplayed the importance of personal computing for years after Apple got that ball rolling in 1976.

---

8 YOUR PROJECTIONS FOR YOUR PRODUCTS' FUTURE

We tend to think that trends, if they are good for our business, will go on forever. If they are bad, we are convinced they will soon turn around. In 1980 and 1981, a decade of Middle East turmoil had crude oil prices at more than $30 a barrel. Planners in the major oil companies agreed unanimously that the rise would continue through the rest of the century. They predicted $50-per-barrel prices in the 1990s. Instead, the prices soon dipped below $20 a barrel and stayed submerged there for most of the next 15 years. The reality that the prognosticators overlooked was that consumers, especially the big commercial users, would adapt to the higher prices by learning to conserve and by switching to other fuels.

A company's sense of reality can be a deeply ingrained part of its culture—the common beliefs and assumptions its people share. These beliefs and assumptions become the conventional wisdom, the *right* way to think about things. If that culture says that the mainframe computer will dominate forever or that foreign competition doesn't matter, if it discourages challenging assumptions, the company will hold on to that belief until it cannot escape reality. And by then, of course, it will have lost a lot of ground.

The Biggest Block to Truth: Fear

Why is it so hard to see reality? Some of the reasons stem from simple human nature—the way people overestimate their own strengths and underestimate their weaknesses. Every successful local sports bookie understands how this tendency extends to organizations. Bookies adjust the odds on games in any locality to take advantage of bettors' overconfidence in or sentimental devotion to the home team.

Although business executives cannot change human nature, they can adjust for it by instilling a healthy skepticism toward predictions of success. They *can*, in other words, change the organizational impediments to seeing reality.

The biggest of these is fear—fear of change, of disagreement, and especially of the boss's wrath. Mid-level managers may be justifiably afraid to challenge their bosses' sense of reality. After all, the senior managers brought the organization to where it is. If the current reality is unpleasant, they may not want to hear it. They may want to shoot the messenger bearing bad news.

William Agee, former chairman and CEO of Morrison Knudsen Corporation, reportedly browbeat his strategic planners until they gave him the projections he wanted, and he fired those who wouldn't provide the figures to justify his programs. This is an extreme case, but insidious versions of the same thing plague many companies. At budget time, middle managers and division heads may try to produce realistic sales and expense forecasts only to be told that level of performance isn't good enough. The numbers are changed, and senior managers feel as though they have accomplished something.

In truth, such forecasts are only numbers on a piece of paper. In the end, reality gets in the way of forecasts no matter how many levels of management have endorsed them. Reality caught up with Morrison Knudsen in 1994 when the company suffered a $350 million loss. The board fired Agee in February 1995.

Along with fear of retribution, mid-level executives may avoid reality because they don't want to raise issues they don't have answers for. Their corporate culture has told them: "Don't surface a problem unless you know the solution." No more common corporate "word to the wise" exists, and it's a disaster. The company's managers should seek to surface problems so that people throughout the organization can work together to solve them.

Reality may also bring about threatening changes. An executive in charge of setting up self-directed teams isn't likely to tell top managers that teams aren't working for their organization. He or she might be labeled a failure and fired. This sort of bureaucratic self-protection is one of the reasons why fads last so long once they get started. They have employees behind them who have a vested interest—their jobs—in keeping the fads alive despite the realities.

Intel and GE Have 20/20 Vision

Seeing reality is the starting point for any winning company. It's the foundation on which everything else is built. An organizational change, or any other action, isn't going to help your organization unless it's based on a sound understanding of the realities your business faces. All of the strategic planning and scenario building in the world won't mean a thing if they are not grounded in reality.

Some companies consistently see reality clearly. Andrew Grove, CEO of Intel, has been widely quoted as saying: "Only the paranoid survive." I think what he means, in a bit of hyperbole, is that you'd better be constantly vigilant to what's going on in the marketplace or you won't last. Real paranoids don't have a good grasp on reality. Grove does, as proven by the ninefold increase in revenues he has achieved for Intel over the course of nine years. No one sees the computer industry and his company's role in it better, unless it's William Gates, chairman and CEO of Microsoft.

Another well-known practitioner of reality-based management is Jack Welch, chairman and CEO of General Electric. When he took the top job at that company in 1981, he inherited 200 strategic planners. Filtering the facts through so many sets of eyes did little to produce an accurate image of GE's reality.

At the time, GE had 43 strategic business units (SBUs), each with a planning staff that produced an elaborate document once a year—its strategic plan. Those 43 SBUs reported to six sectors, each with a planning staff that produced its own document. All 49 documents went to a corporate planning department, which reviewed the plans and prepared them for presentation to Reginald Jones, the CEO who preceded Welch.

Welch immediately recognized a reality that others had overlooked: There were too many planners spending far too much of the company's time and effort cranking out paper. Welch believed the process, which had once produced useful strategies, now was bureaucratic, cumbersome, and inhibiting.

After cutting the planning staff in half and doing away with all reviews involving one set of planners talking to another, Welch conducted the planning reviews with his two

vice-chairmen and the people who actually ran the businesses, who used their planning staffs for support. He also
disbanded the six sectors as an unnecessary layer of management and reduced the major business units from 43 to 15.

The result, I believe, is a company that sees reality much
more clearly than one with hundreds of planners building
their own bureaucracy.

Turning Ugly Realities into Inviting Prospects

Part of getting real is acknowledging problems promptly. I
learned that lesson myself in 1987 when I was part of a group
that conducted a small leveraged buyout.

We bought a company called Bach Engineering, a manufacturer and seller to the airlines of "passenger control
units," the panels that allow passengers to dial audio
stations, control the volume, turn the lights on, and call the
flight attendant. With $3 million in annual revenue, Bach
was ranked third in market share. We were attracted to
Bach because its business was quality-intensive, service-
oriented, and relatively free from fierce price competition
and high technological demands—or so we thought.

This was our second leveraged buyout. Our first had gone
exactly as planned, but this one was different. Within six
months of making the purchase, we realized that the reality
was changing rapidly from what we believed it would be.
Two expensive technological changes were about to envelope
this industry: The major airlines planned to switch from ana-
log to digital control units and to introduce in-seat video.

While both of these changes represented greater market
opportunities for Bach, they put us in a tight financial bind.
We had to keep margins high and use the cash coming in to
pay the debt from the purchase. We couldn't make our debt
payments and afford the investments needed to incorporate

both digital and video technologies. In fact, a hard look at the reality suggested that even a company with little debt would have trouble making those investments unless it had more market share than our company did. In other words, the companies ranked first and second could afford the technological changes; we could not.

This reality was ugly. If we had ignored it and stuck to running the business following our original plan, some two or three years down the line we would have to confront product obsolescence. The market would have long since passed us by. I think that the loan guarantees many of us had personally made helped us focus on seeing reality clearly and finding a solution.

Our analysis produced two conclusions essential to our survival: First, we needed a much larger market share than our current 20 percent. Second, the changes coming in our industry meant that no company could compete with a highly leveraged balance sheet. We needed less debt and more equity capital. We needed to be bigger, to take the company public, and to pay down our debt with the money we would raise from a public offering.

By facing up to the reality and analyzing the situation correctly, we identified a solution: We would buy one of our competitors. Next came a stroke of luck that enabled us to implement our solution. The No. 2 player in the industry was a company called EECO Avionics. Although it was twice our size, it was just a small and out-of-place division of a conglomerate with its own problems. The parent company, suffering through a slump, couldn't afford the technological changes the market forced on us all. Besides, it needed to raise cash by selling some assets, which gave us an opportunity.

Using short-term financing, we bought EECO Avionics. Overnight, we became three times our former size and the top competitor in the industry. Then, within 12 months of consummating the acquisition, we took the new company public and used the capital raised to retire its debt.

The company, now called BE Aerospace, has continued to grow, helped along by the acquisition of other companies in the aircraft-interior field over the years. Today it is the acknowledged world leader in products for inside the passenger compartments of aircraft. With almost $250 million a year in revenues, it sells not only video equipment and control units but also seats, galleys, and other items.

Analysts commenting on BE's history often focus on the tools we used—leverage and acquisitions—and ignore the reasons we used them: to solve some tough problems arising from a reality we hadn't anticipated. I think what really gave us the opportunity to save our investment and grow was our ability to see a problem and face up to it early on.

"Truth Week" Helped Chrysler Change

Companies can, of course, change their culture to a more reality-based one. In 1989, Doug Anderson, one of my partners at the Center for Executive Development (CED), helped Chrysler Corporation accomplish this transformation. At the time, Chrysler was a company adrift. After a wave of acquisitions that included Gulfstream Aerospace (corporate jets), Electrospace Systems (defense), E. F. Hutton Credit and Finance America (finance), and the Thrifty, Snappy, Dollar, and General car rental outfits, Chrysler had lost its focus on its core car and truck business. Its profits were suffering.

To their credit, Lee Iacocca and his top managers began to see the reality: The company's lackluster performance was related to its unfocused internal culture. They called CED in to help change the culture.

Iacocca and his managers explained that, after seven good years for the auto industry, they were expecting a recession and a decline in total demand over the next few years.

Compounding the problem, Chrysler's share of the market was expected to drop because it had no new products scheduled to come out until at least 1992. One result of Chrysler's unfocused culture, then, was going to be an obsolete product lineup.

In the capital-intensive auto industry, where high sales are needed just to break even, lower demand and smaller market share would lead Chrysler to substantial losses, perhaps even to bankruptcy. A decade earlier when Chrysler was in crisis, Iacocca overcame the trouble in large part through personal leadership, including his famous appeal to the federal government for loan guarantees. Iacocca told us he was absolutely convinced that this time the company's revival would have to be led by the entire management team.

Since a clear view of reality needs to precede any constructive action, what Chrysler most needed from us was help with a move to a reality-based culture. Iacocca was beginning to see the problem clearly; now the rest of the company needed to hear—and accept—the message. Moreover, Chrysler had to make sure it saw new realities as they developed. That way it would be less likely to fall into periods of drifting again.

Doug organized and led a series of five-day seminars that the company's top 500 managers attended off-site in groups of 40. These seminars became known as "Truth Week." The participants spent the first two and a half days of the seminar identifying and confronting the realities that the company faced: not only the scary financial possibilities ahead, but also the serious internal problems that had helped lead to them. The internal realities included tremendous distrust and lack of cooperation among the company's departments, a product development cycle that was twice as long as the Japanese standard, and an organization that felt disenfranchised and ineffective.

In the first half of Truth Week, we made presentations to the managers and gave them examples of what happened to some companies that didn't confront their realities. During this stage, the participants broke into groups of six or eight to identify the realities they felt Chrysler wasn't facing up to. These candid sessions produced a high level of agreement on the most critical issues for Chrysler.

Identify Problems, and Solutions Will Follow

Such a high level of consensus might seem surprising at first, but it is my experience that once you create an atmosphere of candor in a company, it doesn't take long for the managers—who are by and large intelligent and motivated—to identify and agree on the real issues they have to confront. And once you're clear on the problems, the solutions will follow.

At Chrysler, in fact, solutions did follow in the second half of the program, when the managers developed action plans for dealing with the major issues they had identified. At the conclusion of Truth Week, the participants made a presentation to Iacocca or one of the other two members of the Office of the Chairman on the issues identified and the actions recommended.

I can give two examples of how Truth Week helped with specific problems. The first deals with the need to cut costs.

Since it was too late for Chrysler to create new and exciting products that would increase sales in the short term, the company needed to spend less to survive the coming financial crisis—$1 billion less. That was evident to the participants. It also became clear to them that the way Chrysler had reduced costs in the past just wasn't good enough.

In the auto industry's boom-and-bust cycle, managers had grown accustomed to periodic across-the-board cuts in personnel according to a mandated percentage. The seminar participants evaluated this situation for what it really was: In good times, managers hired extra people only to lay them off during the inevitable bad times. Once that fact was out on the table, we could confront the truth and ask Truth Week participants how much expense they could really eliminate if they thought about the problem differently. Instead of thinking in terms of reducing head count by a fixed percentage throughout the company, we asked them how much they could save by reducing or eliminating any activities that weren't essential for the successful management of the company. We call this approach *strategic expense reduction*.

When Iacocca learned that our Truth Week participants thought that they could cut even more than $1 billion from expenses if they attacked the problem strategically, he made them a proposal: He'd hold 10 percent of the salary of those 500 managers in escrow. If they failed to achieve $1 billion in cost reductions over three years, they would forfeit the money. If they met or exceeded the goal, they would get the money back with a bonus. The result: Over the next three years Chrysler eliminated $3 billion from expenses, and the managers received a return two and a half times the amount they had withheld.

I have been involved in many downsizings, and in almost every case the savings achieved are less than what management called for. What Chrysler achieved—triple the goal —demonstrates what you can do when you unleash the power that comes from confronting reality.

Another problem the Chrysler executives identified and worked on during Truth Week was the company's long development cycle. Our case studies showed that sometimes Chrysler spent twice as long to develop a new model as the Japanese automakers did. When we asked why the development cycle took so long, participants in the group sessions pointed to a lack of cooperation among departments: Engineering didn't coordinate well with manufacturing;

neither got along with marketing. The failure to coordinate development meant wasted time and a need for intervention from top management. When senior managers resolved disputes, they often reversed decisions that had already cost months of wasted time and millions of dollars.

For this problem, the Truth Week participants proposed, and top management accepted, another dramatic solution. Chrysler did away with the type of organizational structure it had always had—a functional one in which people are organized by the kind of work they do. Instead of reporting to an all-powerful engineering department—manufacturing, marketing, and so on—employees now would join one of four platform teams. Each team engaged in all the functions needed to produce and bring to market a new car for its platform or size category. The change obliterated functional lines.

Today, Chrysler has the fastest and least expensive product development cycle in the auto industry worldwide. The platform teams make all necessary decisions. Chrysler's current chairman and CEO, Robert Eaton, has commented that he has not needed to intervene in a product decision since he took office in 1992.

Chrysler's Truth Week is a dramatic example of how an organization can become reality-based. It often requires someone from the outside—a consultant or facilitator—to provide an unbiased view. A period of reflection off-site, far away from the business's turf and pressures, is also helpful. Even more important, though, is a commitment on the part of senior managers to be part of the process. Over the years, I have turned down the requests of potential clients if I determined that their senior managers believe change is necessary for the *other* people in their organization.

Confronting reality requires the efforts of everyone in the organization, from top to bottom.

Toolbox for Getting Real

What tools can you use once your organization has made a commitment to seeing reality clearly? I'd recommend these:

◆ Make a personal commitment to get real, no matter how painful it may be to face the truth. Encourage everyone in your organization to follow your example.

◆ Call a meeting for the workers in a department or business unit where the price of admission is a written list of three realities the company isn't facing adequately. Discuss the problems openly.

◆ Conduct a meeting where the price of admission is a written list of three reasons why your company won't succeed or why your department won't meet its objectives. This gets potentially painful realities out on the table.

◆ Consider the kind of Truth Week that worked for Chrysler.

◆ Maintain an in with the outs, to borrow a phrase from de Gaulle's four rules of leadership. In any established organization, you can find bright, perceptive people who have been passed over for promotions even though they possess a good sense of what's going on. Maybe they have personality problems or lack management skills. Great leaders find these people and encourage their insights. They have less to lose in telling the truth than managers with a vested interest.

♦ If your company is publicly held, get the reports of securities analysts on your organization and industry. Circulate them widely around the company. Almost invariably, some will be negative. You don't need to kowtow to Wall Street, but you should do everything you can to understand what flaws an analyst sees. Sometimes, when I conduct seminars with a particularly frozen management group, I bring in a securities analyst with negative views to discuss them.

♦ Conduct a relentless search for information on the size and boundaries of your market and your share of it.

♦ Find out how satisfied your customers are and why your noncustomers aren't doing business with you.

♦ Determine how your costs compare with your competitors' and whether you are using current technology to reign in expenses.

With some of these tools, you may need outside help. If you are sure you can do it without hiring consultants, that's great. Remember, though, that the insiders with the biggest offices are the ones who brought the company to where it is. They may feel threatened by fresh views, and others may be afraid to tell them what's really going on. If that sounds like your company, you may need a consultant to get at the facts or a facilitator to serve as an honest broker to assure that people can speak freely.

Consider outside help, too, if you need to conduct consumer surveys. When companies do their own surveying, they tend to get the answers they want, accurate or not. Also, in industries where competitive information is hard to come by, you may need an outsider to dig out facts or to arrange benchmarking.

The role of a consultant in these exercises is not to tell you how to solve your problems. You and your people can do a better job of that. A consultant can help you get good information from both inside and outside whose flow to you has been blocked.

Once you have examined the organization from the bottom up, you can reverse the hydraulic lift and let its wheels touch real ground. Now you are ready to start your engines and *Get Moving!*

2

Principle Two

GET MOVING

How to study a problem only long enough to solve it, accept that mistakes will be made, avoid witch-hunts, and cure analysis paralysis.

How to recognize that the risks of doing nothing are often greater than the risks of making mistakes.

Walk in to any electronics store, and you'll see names like Aiwa, Daewoo, Hitachi, Nokia, Sony, and Toshiba. Roam the parking lot at a shopping mall; you'll no doubt find BMWs, Hondas, Hyundais, Mazdas, Nissans, Toyotas, Volkswagens, and Volvos. Now look at the major appliances in your home—the refrigerator, range, and dishwasher in your kitchen, your washer and dryer, your air conditioner. The chances are close to 100 percent that they bear the brand of U.S. manufacturers.

Why hasn't foreign competition made the same inroads

on our major appliance markets as it has on our car and stereo markets over the last 30 years or so?

The answer is that two American companies—General Electric and Whirlpool—got real and got moving when it counted. In the early and mid-1970s, each of these companies, acting independently, began taking hard looks at what foreign competition could do to them. They learned that, at the time, it cost Japanese companies slightly more than it cost them to make major appliances. The trouble was, though, that costs for Japanese manufacturers were steadily declining, whereas those in the United States were climbing just as steadily.

Both GE and Whirlpool mastered the first principle, *Get Real*. They faced reality and saw that if the current trends continued, Japanese manufacturers could make major appliances and ship them to the United States cheaper than GE and Whirlpool could afford to sell them. Now it was time for the second principle, *Get Moving*. GE and Whirlpool couldn't stop costs from declining for the Japanese; their only hope was to reverse the direction of their own costs.

From that time on, as American automakers and other manufacturers lost ground rapidly to low-cost imports, GE and Whirlpool established—and achieved—the goal of maintaining their cost advantage. Both companies stopped the practice of planning their expenses by looking at the past and adding a factor for inflation. That wasn't going to work in an environment where competitors were bringing their expenses down.

Instead, the appliance makers decided to revolutionize how they manufacture. GE, for example, spent $38 million to make the dishwasher line at its Appliance Park facilities in Louisville, Kentucky, a model of high-tech, low-cost manufacturing. It replaced 60 percent of the equipment on the line with the latest, most efficient machinery.

Once the three-year project was completed, robots carried out the more repetitive jobs, reducing manpower needs by about half. GE redesigned the manufacturing process so that it could be done with 78 percent fewer parts. The required parts are actually manufactured at nine points along the line and used immediately. That's the ultimate just-in-time inventory system.

The overall cost reduction was 10 percent, but GE also took advantage of the redesign to implement a number of quality improvements. The new assembly line gives the employees at each workstation as much time as they need to complete their job satisfactorily or divert faulty units to a rework station.

When GE completed the redesign of the line in the early 1980s, it was considered the "factory of the future" and became a model for other GE operations. It also was a visible testament to acting on the reality that corporate managers have identified.

This is perhaps the most important of the six principles. We know from the previous chapter that seeing reality—*getting real*—doesn't come easy. But even the clearest of visions will take you nowhere if you don't actually get moving. This may sound obvious, but look at the brand names that have disappeared from your home: Admiral, Frigidaire, Gibson, Norge, Westinghouse.

While GE and Whirlpool worked furiously to maintain their cost advantage and stave off foreign competition, these other companies seemed to think their inalienable right as American appliance manufacturers would protect them from harm. As the other companies fell, GE's market share in major appliances increased significantly from 1975 to 1986, as did Whirlpool's.

Why Analyzing Takes Priority over Doing

In my work as a consultant, I've been dumbfounded at the number of companies that can't seem to act, even in the light of clear market signals that they must. Often, the middle-level managers are frustrated by the paralysis at the senior level. It seems as though going to meetings and studying a problem takes priority over doing something about it.

Why don't organizations take action? Once again, fear is a major reason. Taking action means that you may be held accountable for the result. If things don't go your way, the course you selected will have your name clearly posted on it. To a fearful executive, it seems safer to study the issue and seek a consensus with others before committing to a decision. "Look before you leap" prevails over "He who hesitates is lost." But "looking"—analysis and consensus formation—may go on forever and usually does.

A second fear is simply the fear of change we discussed in the last chapter. It is hardly unreasonable. When GE considered redesigning its dishwasher line, it was clear that some jobs would disappear and others would be redefined in such a way as to require many workers to be retrained in more complex tasks. Managers, too, would need to learn new methods to supervise their employees. It might have seemed tempting to avoid the whole thing, but GE saw the need and made the commitment to change.

Another major impediment to action is perfectionism. Corporate cultures often grow up around perfectionist ideals. Everything must be 100 percent this or that, with no exceptions. Inevitably, such an atmosphere lifts a mere fear of accepting responsibility into sheer terror. Nothing gets done because the corporate culture demands the perfect answer, which of course never comes. Thus people come to believe that going to meetings is actually doing something. Of course, just as some "looking" is right and necessary before you leap, so some ideals of perfection are right and necessary to produce something good or better. But if you wait for perfect certainty or perfect anything else, you'll never, ever *get moving*.

You can easily tell a paralyzing culture when executives spend as much time evaluating their everyday decisions as they do major investment shifts. I've known organizations where it takes the professional staff five or six meetings over several months to make a small realignment of secretarial responsibilities.

The third impediment to action that I'll mention here is the belief that any decision worth making is worth making ten times. In companies suffering from this malady, as soon as people decide on a course of action and take their first tentative steps, they begin a reappraisal and set off in an entirely different direction.

When I consulted for Digital Equipment Corporation in the late 1980s, the company had a culture of teams and committees that held endless meetings. We would discuss a course of action, people would say yes, and then later I would learn that we hadn't committed to the action at all. The company even had a name for the decision that wasn't really a decision at all. When I pointed out that I thought everyone had agreed, I was told, "Oh, that was the 'DEC nod.' We all know the decision will be revisited."

The 80 Percent Solution

One CEO I have worked with tells his employees to study a problem until they are 80 percent sure of the solution, then get moving on implementation. That's good advice.

In that CEO's company, it's safe to assume that people will make decisions that aren't perfect 20 percent of the time. Maybe the decision will be fundamentally right but flawed. Next is the problem of identifying the one error out of every five and fixing it. When his people are 80 percent certain that they have the right fix, again they implement it. Note that they never quite get to 100 percent. But that's okay: They are always getting closer. As Piet Hein once wrote:

The road to wisdom?
Well, it's plain and simple to express:
Err and err and err again,
But less and less and less.

Bear that in mind, and you'll have found one way to keep your culture action-based. The precise math isn't important. What *is* important is acknowledging that any action is less than perfect but that moving forward usually beats standing still.

Admitting mistakes is painful, but to foster an action orientation in your company, you will need to take some of the sting out. A group of investors that I belong to felt the pain of making mistakes after we had bought a company called Applied Extrusion Technology in 1986 and merged it with another company in 1990. Based on four smooth and successful years of experience, we made two assumptions about the combination—that there were significant savings to be made by consolidating two plants into one, and that we could develop a new product for use in landfills. We thought we had a breakthrough technology for a product that would prevent contaminated materials from leaching in landfills.

We invested a lot of money in consolidating the plants and developing the product. It turned out that we were wrong in both cases. The cost savings weren't there, and the new product was not as much of a breakthrough as we thought. Admitting the error was painful, but we did and moved on to other projects and new priorities. As we recognized that our efforts were just plain falling short and our priorities shifted, we ended up acquiring another business that had better growth potential.

One large company that has maintained an action-based orientation is Minnesota Mining and Manufacturing. William McKnight, who led 3M from 1929 to 1966, built the culture that guides the company to this day. Long before the word "empowerment" was fashionable, McKnight said: "Those men to whom we delegate authority and responsibility, if they are good men, are going to have ideas of their own and are going to want to do their jobs their own way. These are characteristics we want in men and should be encouraged. Mistakes will be made, but [these] are not so serious in the long run as the mistakes management makes if it is dictatorial."

McKnight also was responsible for the policy that lets 3M researchers spend 15 percent of their time working on the project of their choosing. That policy along with 3M's acceptance of mistakes and its action orientation led to one of the most successful new products of the 1980s—Post-it Notes.

Spencer Silver, a 3M scientist, was trying to develop a super-strong adhesive in the 1970s when he came up with just what he *wasn't* looking for—a low-tack glue that would stick to things but not bond tightly. Before calling it a total failure, he showed it to his colleagues, none of whom could think of a use for it—at least not right away.

One Sunday, though, as chemical engineer Arthur Fry was singing in his church choir, he grew annoyed with the way the bookmarks kept falling out of place in his hymnal. Wishing for a bookmark that would stay in place, he suddenly remembered the "mistake" Silver had shown him. Fry then decided to devote his "bootlegging" time—the 15 percent he could control—to working with the low-tack glue.

It took Fry four years of experimenting, but eventually he perfected the glue so that it would hold notes to paper but then not make tears when pulled off. What's more, the notes could be repositioned. When he showed it to the marketers, though, they told him there would be no buyers for it. While the test marketing bore out the marketers' low expectations, someone noticed that when samples were made available, the Post-it Notes disappeared in a hurry. It's become one of those products that answered a need consumers didn't realize they had.

Fortunately for 3M, the company culture gave both Silver and the marketers room to make mistakes and empowered Fry to act on his beliefs. The resulting product, rolled out nationally in 1980, has brought 3M immeasurable success not only in the product's ingenuity and application but in the extended diversity of Post-it Notes now available.

In the last ten years or so, many companies have adopted a team-based culture. The office staff at my executive education and consulting company administers itself as a team. With teams, though, you have to be even more vigilant that you don't fall into inactivity. People start thinking that they have to make decisions by consensus—with lots of meetings until *everyone* agrees on the action to take. There's nothing more deadly to getting things done.

In an action-based organization, you will assign to teams those projects that will benefit from a multidisciplinary approach. And you will hold the teams to a schedule for action. A company like GE might very well use a team—with members from engineering, manufacturing, and marketing— to design a new refrigerator. If you find yourself going to meetings to hammer out a position on lunch schedules, your team approach has gone awry. Some decisions cry out to be *made*, not discussed.

Management Appreciation vs. Management Action

The tendency to analyze rather than act may be aggravated by the high rate at which universities are turning out MBAs and companies are hiring them. The number of MBA graduates in the United States grew from 5,000 to 75,000 from 1970 to 1995, and business schools tend to mold superb analysts. They teach what I call *management appreciation* at the expense of *manage-ment action.* As I've said, there is a place for analysis, but organizations also need doers at the top to maintain balance.

Here's what I mean by management appreciation versus management action: In the 1970s and early 1980s, the story of the Progressive Corporation was a classic case study used in business schools. Progressive, an automobile insurance com-pany, thought that it was too small to compete with the giants—Allstate, State Farm, and others. The company carved out a niche for itself by selling its insurance to the drivers the big companies didn't want—those considered high-risk.

Progressive focused on just 15 percent of the total market. Those drivers, rejected by other insurance companies, were willing to pay hefty premiums, which more than covered Progressive's high costs. In 1980, Progressive was 48th in size among auto insurers but first in profitability.

Business school students were asked to appreciate Progressive's strategy. Teachers and students assumed that the big guys would never invade Progressive's niche and that Progressive could never compete with the big guys by offer-ing a full range of auto insurance. Business schools were teaching appreciation for a strategy that was static.

In the 1980s, Allstate and State Farm did, in fact, begin to envy Progressive's high-margin niche and offer policies to high-risk drivers. Since their overall cost base was lower than Progressive's, they could undersell the smaller company and take a big chunk of its niche. At the same time, punitive legislation in California cost Progressive millions. It was enough to paralyze most companies, but this story has a happy ending. Progressive worked on management action, not management appreciation.

Progressive's chairman and CEO, Peter Lewis, got real and got moving. Seeing the environment as it was, not as he wished it were, he decided that auto insurance *was* overpriced and that insurers probably deserved their miserable reputation. He began competing with the big guys across the board. Lewis attacked his company's costs and has succeeded in bringing them down from 33.2 percent of sales to 22.4 percent. That's one percentage point below Allstate's.

Meanwhile, Progressive completely revamped its claims service, moving to a system of 24-hour claims reporting and attempting to settle claims within 24 hours. Whereas in 1988 it took an average of five days before a claims representative even got to the policyholder, in 1996 some 80 percent of all claims were settled within 24 hours. Often, the claims adjuster shows up at the scene of the accident. This policy had a two-pronged positive effect: In addition to improving customer relations, the quick response stems fraudulent claims.

Guess what happened to the company that used to be a small but profitable niche player. It is now a big and profitable insurance company—the sixth largest U.S. auto insurer, with a return on equity of more than 20 percent.

Progressive's story is an example of what a company can do when its leadership is willing to face reality and act on it. Analysis, of course, is important. Learning why a company is successful at any given time can hone a student's analytic skill, but success calls for acting decisively as well as seeing clearly.

A Tale of Two Companies: Microsoft and Wang

Perhaps one of the greatest examples of decisive business action during the last half of the twentieth century took place in the winter of 1974, when Bill Gates was a Harvard College student and his friend Paul Allen worked for Honeywell in the Boston area. They had previously run a computer-oriented company together, but now an article in *Popular Electronics* would point them toward the business that would bring them billions of dollars ultimately and change the way we all live.

The magazine article, "World's First Minicomputer Kit to Rival Commercial Models," unveiled the MITS Altair 8800. This kit would enable electronics junkies to build a small computer in their homes. At the time, few people realized that there would be a market some day for computers in the home. Analysts at IBM and the other computer giants certainly didn't think so, but Allen and Gates understood what home computers could do.

Gates dropped out of Harvard, Allen left his job, and the two formed Microsoft to supply the programming language hobbyists would need to make the new computer work for them. The story, which began because Gates and Allen sized up reality and took action, is well known. The company grew modestly until 1980, when it won the contract to supply the operating system for IBM's new personal computer, and then its growth skyrocketed.

In the 1970s, as Gates and Allen were seeing their potential, Wang Laboratories was failing to take action on its potential. At the time, the Wang word processor was rapidly replacing the typewriter. This was a machine that encased a keyboard, a video screen, and a printer that did no tasks other than processing words. For a while, it appeared that "the Wang" was going to be to word processing what the "Xerox machine" was to photocopying. Gates and Allen incorporated some of Wang's features into the software they were developing.

Wang failed to see or to act on what was clear to Microsoft: The growth product was the personal computer (PC) and the software that would make it work. Word processing was one of many tasks that a PC could do. As the price of PCs fell, there would be little or no market left for dedicated word processors like Wang's. By the early 1980s, this should have been obvious, but Wang failed to produce the new and more versatile software or hardware that might have competed in the new environment. If Wang had, in fact, confronted its changing market sooner and taken appropriate action, we might be writing and editing on WangWord software instead of Microsoft Word today, or perhaps even working our Microsoft Excel spreadsheets on Wang PCs.

Rounded Bumpers or Square?

In the last chapter we saw how "Truth Week" helped Chrysler speed up its new-product development cycle. But it wasn't just Chrysler that needed to start moving faster, of course. The problem belonged to the entire U.S. auto industry. In studies conducted independently at Harvard Business School and MIT, it was found that it took U.S. companies up to a year and a half longer than Japanese companies to come out with a new car model. The Japanese could do it in around three and a half years.

This time differential hurt U.S. automakers. No one knows what the motorist will want two or three years in the future. What automakers have to do is take their best shot, get the cars into showrooms, and find out what will sell.

Why did it take U.S. companies so much longer? These automobile studies sought the answer. It turned out that the Japanese engineers were no smarter than their American counterparts; they possessed no better computers, and it took them just as long to do the actual development work. The difference lay entirely in the decision-making process.

Here's how it worked: Both U.S. and Japanese companies spent, say, nine or ten months planning the new car and conducting market research. They decided the car's price, features, and look, and then farmed out the engineering work. That's where the difference came in. The Japanese companies said, "Okay, we've made the decision. Now we've got 14 months to complete the engineering and get the new model onto the assembly line." The car materialized on schedule, and the company learned quickly whether it was a hit.

In the U.S., after the development team decided on the price, features, and look, the engineers went to work ordering the dies and tools they needed—reconfiguring an assembly line. Several expensive months later, the CEO would call one of the engineers to say that he had noticed in parking lots that the trend was leaning toward rounded bumpers instead of square ones, or vice versa. To be accommodating, everyone would go back to the drawing board.

Since motorists change their tastes from year to year, the American top brass always had an opportunity to revisit the design question, while the Japanese company stuck to its commitment to get the new model out on time. In the end, according to the studies, neither the Americans nor the Japanese had an edge in deciding what motorists would want—a process that was essentially guesswork anyway. The success and failure rates were about the same for each. The Japanese, however, got more new models to market. So even though the success rate was the same, they ended up with more winners.

The U.S. automakers eventually brought their development time down. How Chrysler did it is outlined in the last chapter. Essentially, the U.S. companies recognized that getting the new model to market takes priority over agonizing about the details.

Ready, Fire, Aim, Aim, Aim

The military, with its modern "smart" bombs, provides a metaphor for this need to put action first. The key phrase has become "ready, fire, aim, aim, aim." The laser-guided bombs don't depend on gravity to get to the target, so "ready, aim, fire" has been relegated to the past. Now the crew on the jet or submarine prepares the missile, fires it, and it checks and rechecks its trajectory, aiming itself as it goes along.

That's what the automakers had to do: Get the model off the assembly line, see how the public reacts, and make adjustments. That's what all action-oriented organizations do. They will spend some time preparing—maybe enough to be 80 percent convinced they are doing the right thing—and then act. Once they get moving and see the results, they will make the adjustments they need to: "Ready, fire, aim, aim, aim."

Toolbox to Get Moving

What can you do to make your organization an action-based one?

◆ Create a decision process. Any time you have issues to resolve, make it clear what decisions you need to make before you can commit to action, then stay focused on those decisions. Call the question each time you have a meeting on these issues. By that I mean, ask yourselves whether you have enough information to make a decision. If the answer is yes, you have done your job. If the answer is no, determine what additional information you need and get it. What you're aiming for here is to have a decision process that results in decisions, not more meetings and endless analysis.

◆ Make sure any study or task force you organize has an action-based mission. It isn't just gathering data. If the group doesn't know what action can result from the information it is collecting, then it probably shouldn't be meeting. Consulting at various companies over the years, I have often been astounded at how people run from one meeting to another. I ask: "What is the purpose of this task group? What problem are you trying to solve? What decision is likely to result from your meeting?" Often the answer is: "Beats me." The meetings have taken on a life of their own.

◆ Outlaw any meeting that doesn't have a clear purpose, agenda, and fixed length. Endless meetings are a sure sign of a company mired in inactivity.

◆ Create an *action-agenda workshop*. This is a meeting, open to all of your organization's staff members, where the price of admission is a list of at least three key items your company or organization isn't acting on. To keep the meeting from becoming a gripe session, ask the participants to include one or two steps that they would recommend to get moving on these items.

◆ Spread the word in your organization that you expect people to act when they are 80 percent sure that they are right.

◆ Spread the word also that it is okay to make a few mistakes as long as people act promptly to fix them. Companies often get bogged down in fretting over mistakes and conducting witch-hunts to assess blame. The important thing is to understand the cause and get on with the remedy.

Admitting mistakes requires a willingness to be honest, which is the subject of the third principle: *Speak the Truth.*

3

Principle Three

SPEAK THE TRUTH

*How to be straight with employees,
and have them talk straight to you.*

*How unclear, guarded, and dishonest behavior
can be much more damaging than painful truth.*

After the AT&T divestiture several years ago, the leaders
of one of the large telecommunications companies created
in its wake called me in to help them institute a cultural change
in one of their biggest business groups. They wanted me to
conduct a training program for all middle managers in the
new organization.

The company had coasted for a long time as a "nice place to work." People didn't confront one another, so nonperformers rarely heard that they weren't contributing. As long as the business environment was benign, the company could get by, even with a padded workforce.

As with so many other companies in recent years, however, the firm's environment was becoming more competitive. It couldn't afford the padding anymore. The managers had to get the message that the culture would change. They needed to recognize what the changes would be and then acquire the skills necessary to make the transition.

I felt, and the company leaders agreed, that roughly a third of the managers had already gotten the message and had the skills they needed. Another third had the right attitude; with proper training they could understand what the changes are and could pick up the appropriate skills. The last third were more set in their ways. We all had our doubts about whether they would ever hear the message and, even if they did, whether they would be able to change.

I thought to myself, "Okay, the first third is a done deal. And if I'm good, I should be able to get the middle third on board—no one can bat a thousand, but I should be able to get close to it. The challenging group is the bottom third. We can't just give up on them. If I can get 25 percent of them, that's great work."

I was thinking of ways to improve the success rate of the program. I became convinced that we would do better if the company leaders leveled with the participants on the first day of training. I wanted the executives to just lay the situation calmly out on the table—that if the managers did not make the transition, they weren't going to make it in this company. I also wanted them to say, "The way we assess it, we think perhaps a third of you may not make it. Prove us wrong." This would certainly motivate everyone in the middle third and many of the people in the bottom third. Besides, it would be fairer to tell everyone up front how serious the situation was.

I presented this idea to the company leaders. They said, "No, that's too brutal." I just stood there. "What's brutal about telling the truth?" I objected. They vetoed the idea.

Without the stronger medicine, the program went as I expected: The first third was fine. The middle third made a lot of progress. The last third never really tuned in to the message. Sure enough, many in that last group eventually lost their jobs—not through attrition but in a series of layoffs that made local news. Needless to say, the layoffs were much more upsetting than the truth would have been. Honesty would have brought more senior managers on board and would have helped the company change faster. Faster change would have led to greater competitive success, reducing the need for layoffs. Honesty would have led the company along a more successful path—and one with less serious consequences.

Being honest doesn't preclude being nice. Furthermore, most people prefer the truth to platitudes, even if it makes them momentarily uncomfortable. That's what my third principle of winning management, *Speak the Truth*, is about. It is nothing more than having an organization in which people, in a straightforward way, say what is on their minds without fear of recrimination. It is about honesty and openness at four levels:

- ◆ From supervisors to employees, with frank assessments of performance and suggestions for change.

- ◆ From the company to its workforce, about the state of the business and what that means for employees.

- ◆ From workers to their superiors, when they think their bosses are making a mistake.

- ◆ From peers to peers, about conflicts or disagreements that might hamper their work.

Of course, these notions are simple to express. They are very hard to put into practice.

Speak the Truth is the first of what might be called the "softer" principles of good management. Most businesspeople like to focus on formulating strategy and acting on it. They neglect the issues that are less tangible, like communication, vision, decision-making, and leadership. When they do address these subjects, they do it in an indirect, ineffective way—like sending out superficial newsletters to employees.

Speaking the truth has two components: honesty and openness. There is a subtle difference between the two. To be honest means that there can be no posturing, no careful selection of words. Discussions are candid. To be open means that all issues can be raised. A company needs both forms of telling the truth. I can tell you everything about the firm's financial statements, but intentionally not discuss downsizing. That's honest but not open.

I have found that the best managers and the most successful companies handle these softer subjects directly and frankly, and with great care and skill. In many ways they are the clearest signs of a winning organization. I'll devote the rest of the book to these often overlooked and mishandled issues, starting with honesty, which I consider the most critical to the quality of work life at a company.

Please note that even though these subjects are "soft," they are fundamental to accomplishing the harder objectives. For example, speaking the truth is absolutely necessary to achieving the principle of getting real. How can you get real if your people are not going to tell you what's going on? If your R&D people are behind in a development project, you need an honest assessment from them of when it will be ready. If they say the product will be on the market in four to six months, it had better be four to six months. If they say four to six months to cover their butts, and it ends up being two years, then you have serious problems. If they had told you the truth, you could have explored alternatives for getting the product to market, such as a joint venture with another company. Speaking the truth may be a "soft" principle, but doing so is hard work.

Talking Face-to-Face

Time and again, executives I work with tell me a common story. At some point when they took over a new department, they inherited a manager whom they saw as weak. Other executives concurred. This assessment seemed strange, however, given that the manager had been with the company for 15 years. So the executive gets the personnel file and finds that the person has gotten consistently high ratings.

Now the executive is in trouble. If he tells the manager, "You aren't performing," the person responds, "I've been here for years and have gotten great reviews. Who do you think you are?" Furthermore, if the executive wants to remove the person, he's on very unsteady ground. There's no documentation of a performance problem.

I don't think the behavioral sciences have a name for this phenomenon, but even the most powerful executives—people who readily make speeches to roomfuls of investment analysts, who testify before Congress, who are able to issue orders that result in thousands of layoffs—cringe at the thought of sitting down with one subordinate to discuss a performance issue.

Honesty and openness between supervisors and employees are required in daily operation. But they are the most difficult to achieve in performance reviews. Even the most straightforward companies struggle with these issues.

Eli Lilly and Company, for example, holds honesty and openness in high regard. At the company's 1995 shareholders meeting, Chairman Randall Tobias gave a rousing address about how the company's most fundamental value is respect for people. Integrity, he said, is key to demonstrating that respect. "Our concept of integrity," he said, "will embrace the very highest benchmarks of honesty, ethical behavior, and exemplary moral character in all we do." Wishing to build on these established values to make them more contemporary, Tobias noted that integrity also required "consistently open and honest communication . . . with all our stakeholders and, importantly, with each other." Under Tobias's leadership, the company began to conduct training to help people pick up the behaviors needed for such communication.

Failure to honestly critique an employee's performance hurts the company and the employee. One of Harvard Business School's best-selling case studies poignantly illustrates the message. Peter Browning, an outstanding manager at Continental Can, became president of Continental White Cap, a division that made the tops for ketchup bottles and other similar containers. As the case study explains, White Cap was making money, but it also had a culture of complacency and waste. This loomed as a problem because significant technical innovation was coming soon to the entire cap industry. Continental Can's CEO wanted Browning to wake the place up without upsetting it.

Browning began to assess the division's top people. He found one manager who was seriously underperforming. He asked other executives about the man and heard, "Oh yeah, long-term problem. He's been lost for a while." But when Browning got the manager's personnel file, he found the manager had been rated above average for years.

Browning sat the manager down and told him he had significant problems and had to overcome them in short order because of the division's timetable. Browning also told the manager that his fellow vice presidents had indicated they didn't really respect him. The man was shocked. Browning said, "If you don't believe me, go around and check for yourself." The fellow came back about two weeks later. He told Browning, "What is more disturbing to me than the feedback itself is that no one over the previous 18 years had ever mentioned any of these problems to me."

Browning developed an action plan to help the manager improve, but the fellow couldn't adapt. He was outplaced and ended up doing well in a less demanding job. Browning was not out of the woods, however. Even though he had dealt with the performance problem, he still had to undo a culture built on years of complacency and half-truths.

Unfortunately, many managers endure performance problems because they lack the skills they need to hold straightforward one-on-one conversations. Coaching can help. Managers can role-play conversations or performance reviews with colleagues, a mentor, or a specialist from Human Resources. I have to speak frankly with employees at my own firm from time to time, and I often call in one of my partners to role-play them.

Managers can also bring a third person into an uncomfortable meeting, simply to observe or to act as an honest broker or facilitator. You may think you're being straight with an employee, but the employee may not. The third party can assess how you deliver your message and how the other person receives it.

A more extreme tactic to force no-nonsense performance reviews was used by Andy Pearson, president of PepsiCo until 1985. When he arrived, he found that Pepsi was a soft company. One piece of evidence was the firm's homogeneous performance reviews. He called in the department heads one at a time and told each one, "I want you to rank-order your people." They replied, "What do you mean, 'rank-order'?" Pearson said, "You have 200 people. You've given them all scores of four or five on a five-point scale. They're all great? One of them has to be the best. One has to be the worst. If I tell you that you have to get rid of one person, I assume that'll be the worst one."

Pearson's rule was that unless each division leader had a clear developmental path to improve the bottom 10 percent of their people, those people were gone. At the same time, he wanted a plan for moving each person in the top 10 percent up in the organization. Pearson repeated the exercise each year. As harsh as it was, it transformed the performance review process and improved the frank exchange between supervisors and subordinates.

Having trained many people how to conduct candid performance reviews, I have found that their fear about what may happen by being painfully honest is usually a lot worse than the reality of being so. While the individuals being reviewed may resist the tone at first, they typically end up appreciating the fact that they have been told the truth. And often they are shocked and upset that they were not told the truth sooner.

Failing to give an employee a no-nonsense review in the name of "being nice" doesn't show much respect for that person. Think about it. If you were performing in a way that your boss disliked, would you want him to tell you so you could correct the mistake? Or would you prefer to toil away, unaware that there is a problem?

Jack Stack Opens the Books

While straight talk must take place at an individual level, it also has to happen at an organizational level. The starting point is for chief executives to be straight about the business.

No one could provide greater testimony than Jack Stack. In 1980, International Harvester was a disaster. Before the huge company crumbled, Stack, a plant manager, organized a group of investors to buy out a small engine remanufacturing subsidiary in Missouri, Springfield Remanufacturing Company (SRC). He had to approach dozens of financial institutions before BankAmerica agreed to finance the deal. The bank put up $89 of debt for every $1 of equity—one of the most leveraged buyouts ever.

After its first fiscal year ended in 1984, the Springfield Remanufacturing Company lost $61,000 on sales of $16 million. Costs were far too high. So Stack made a bold move. He opened the company's books—every line item on every spreadsheet—to every employee. He spent more than $100,000 training his employees how to understand the numbers and use them to figure out where to save. Costs began to fall significantly.

The process continues today. Each week plant managers shut down the machines for a half hour while employees break into small groups to study the latest financial statements. They show more than a passing curiosity. In 1995, SRC distributed $1.4 million in bonus pay to 800 employees, all of it linked to how well each division performed against line items such as "profit before taxes." One SRC machinist told *Fortune* magazine, "We know that rebuilding a No. 466 crankshaft is worth $17.60 an hour toward paying for electricity. Yesterday we worked fast enough to pay for an extra $170 in overhead. That kind of effort goes right into our bonus." SRC earned 6 percent pretax in 1995, on sales of $100 million, in an industry where few companies make any margin at all.

Other companies are learning similar lessons. From 1989 to 1991, Mobil Oil was one of the highest-cost producers of crude oil. Management started a program to make all the people on drilling platforms aware of costs, down to the last detail. Within two years Mobil became one of the lowest-cost producers of crude.

The best way to manage bad news is to convey it directly. What breeds so much worker discontent about downsizing, for example, is not the fact that it has to be done. It's when top executives say, "This will be the last cut," and then they make another one. Kodak has done this four or five times. It gets even worse when workers read the next annual report, which makes it sound as if the company's going great guns. You can't have it both ways. When the company doesn't do well, its leaders have to be honest. If they are, they will prevent disillusionment and will set an example that the rest of the company will follow.

Taking this step is important. Many companies do internal surveys to find out if their employees are happy. In my experience, those who get a lot of low scores find that employees' dissatisfaction is ultimately linked to two factors: Employees don't feel that what they're doing is important (we'll get to this in the next chapter on values, purpose, and mission), and they don't think the bosses are shooting straight. There is a lack of trust.

Besides opening the books, company leaders can take other steps to generate an environment that fosters truth. At bottom, you have to convey that the company culture encourages frank discourse. Make it clear that employees won't get their hands slapped if they say something a superior may not want to hear. Managers can reinforce this value by regularly asking certain questions at employee meetings: "Are there issues we're not confronting head-on? Do you think there are areas in which we are not communicating honestly and openly?"

A candid environment can be achieved at a much simpler level, too. It's not an affront for a manager to tell an employee, following a meeting with a customer, that he didn't think the way the employee talked to the customer was professional. But such frankness is missing at most companies. GE's Jack Welch is a big proponent of frank talk. He himself is such a blunt guy that he can be disarming at first. Then you realize, "You know something, he may be blunt, but he's telling me what's on his mind. I prefer that to the suave, debonair type— you can never be quite sure where the person stands." CEO Lawrence Bossidy is trying to encourage similarly open dialogue at AlliedSignal. It doesn't take place everywhere every time yet, but it is wonderful when it occurs.

Talking Back to the Boss

I am often struck by how many seemingly strong men and women balk at the prospect of telling their boss or a group of superiors that they think the company is making a mistake. I don't know whether this difficulty lies in some fear of reprisal or a need to be liked or some deep insecurity. But straight talk must go up the chain of command as well as down.

Admittedly, it is hard for any subordinate to feel comfortable telling his boss bad news or, worse, contradicting his opinions. It will never happen if top managers don't encourage employees to offer their points of view.

For years I have been holding three- to five-day customized seminars on various managerial topics for managers of a given company. They are always sponsored by the CEO, who at the end will come to interact with the participants. The CEO arrives and says, "I'm happy to be here. This program is wonderful. Ask me anything that's on your mind. Don't be afraid to raise the hard questions." He gets hard questions maybe 10 percent of the time. If I've pumped the participants to engage the CEO in a straight conversation, maybe 30 to 40 percent of the questions are tough ones. The rest are softballs. Most people remain convinced that asking tough questions may put their jobs on the line.

After an hour the CEO leaves. He knows he got mostly softballs but seems satisfied. Why?

What's happening most of the time is that a classic co-dependency has developed. Employees have gotten the message over the years that if they ask tough questions, they are doing so at their own risk. The CEOs have convinced themselves that encouraging tough questions somehow undercuts their decision-making authority.

This just isn't the case. It is perfectly okay for employees to ask hard questions or present opinions without implying that they have any say in the final decision on the matter. A company is not a democracy. What does matter, though, is that employees are allowed to express their views. The boss should say to everyone, "Tell me your opinion. I want to hear it and give it full consideration. But in the end, I will decide."

Some CEOs don't want tough questions because they fear they may not know the answer. They are afraid to say "I don't know" because they think that it makes them look weak in public. However, the CEO can say, "Hey, good question. I don't know. I'm going to look into that. Call me Tuesday and we can discuss the answer." This response not only makes the CEO sound honest, it shows leadership from one who respects employees and encourages team play.

Asking questions is one thing. Employees may still refrain from contradicting or criticizing the person who determines their raises. To get around this hesitation, Lawrence Bossidy, CEO at AlliedSignal, holds "skip-level" meetings. People from one level or division, without name tags, come to a conference room and eat lunch with a senior person a few levels up. They sit around talking about what's on their minds. They don't have to worry about reprisal because the senior executive is not going to know their names.

Another tool is *360-degree feedback*. Too often the evaluation of a manager and his leadership role is a subjective and even political process. A process of 360-degree feedback overcomes this. In this scheme, the manager's subordinates, his peers, and his superiors are asked to fill out a performance evaluation. It asks whether the manager has clearly communicated his objectives, whether he gives them a straight story, whether he can be counted on to make good on what he says, and whether they are satisfied with his level of performance.

Constructive contradictions can create superior earnings. Executives at 3M Company encourage employees' willingness to contradict their superiors. It's part of 3M's famous environment for fostering innovation, described in the last chapter. Five times CEO Livio (Desi) DeSimone tried to kill a project aimed at new materials for clothing; each time the project team told him he was stopping them prematurely. The team finally succeeded in developing Thinsulate, one of the most successful insulating materials of all time.

New employees are trained by 3M to take risks, to use objective measures to weigh the likely success of research— and to speak with polite but ruthless candor about their assessments. As a result, the company gets an incredible 30 percent of sales from products that are less than four years old.

Even if employees do learn to be comfortable questioning or challenging a superior, they may find themselves in an even tougher communication situation: How to tell their boss they blew it.

"Blowing it" can take many forms, from offering the wrong product to a customer to running late on a development project. Regardless of the problem, management obviously wants to know about it to help reverse it. Telling employees to come forward is fine, but it will be easier for them if they have been given ways in which they can broach the topic.

One tool I use to solve this communication problem is to write fictitious vignettes about common dilemmas. I pass them out to employees and ask them to comment on how the people in trouble can discuss the problem with their boss. For an example of a vignette I've used in the securities business, see the box on pages 74–76.

Straight Talk with Peers

It's amazing how hard people will work with each other yet not discuss difficult issues that arise between them. This problem is rampant in organizations. If you have a gripe with someone, discuss it directly. Don't go to the person's boss. If I have a problem with Martha and I talk only to her boss about it, I'm not being open with her.

Managers have to try hard not to allow people to avoid each other. Martha's boss should send me to Martha before doing anything and should stay out of the dispute unless the two of us can't work it out. It's the only practice that will encourage a more open working environment. It's like addressing two kids arguing over who's going to control the television: You can break it up, or you can tell them to find a way to work it out themselves.

Managers must realize, however, that it is extremely difficult for some people to confront others in this way, even if they have a legitimate concern. They may need some coaching.

Lack of one-on-one resolution can turn more sinister when two people—say, the heads of finance and manufacturing—bad-mouth each other. Senior managers have to stop this jockeying immediately, or their company will turn into a political organization where finance criticizes manufacturing, manufacturing criticizes sales, and so on. These people have to work together, and they can't if someone's trying to turn one department against another. The point is not that people shouldn't disagree. It's that they should resolve their differences directly and completely, and then lead their people as a team. Substantive issues of conflict are permissible as long as people are willing to get together and reach a resolution.

I was called in to handle this very type of case at a company where I am a director. The president was going to retire within a year, and there were two strong internal candidates to succeed him. The two men were working hard for the job. But board members saw that the two were also competing in some negative and political ways—by not cooperating with each other and creating rivalries between their respective departments.

We brought both of them in for a very candid conversation, telling them that we thought highly of both of them. We then stated that we had noted that there was infighting going on as a result of their potential rise to the top. We told them that if we picked up any signs of political play between the two of them, then *neither* of them would get the president's job. We wouldn't engage in figuring out who was doing it. It was just strictly forbidden.

The infighting stopped immediately. A year later, when we were able to elevate one of them, the other actually ended up staying on in an even stronger role and as part of the executive team. I am convinced that if we had not confronted the situation directly, the jousting would have continued. Then when we promoted one, the animosity that had been created would have caused the other candidate to leave the company and would have left two departments, if not the entire company, in a very bad state of distrust and noncooperation.

Respect for Customers and Shareholders

Let's take honest and open communication one step further: to the customer. The lessons are exactly the same, as the famous Tylenol case proves.

In 1982, eight consumers died after taking Tylenol that had been poisoned. Johnson & Johnson immediately pulled all Tylenol products from the shelves, nationwide. When asked about this years later, James Burke, chairman and CEO, acknowledged that the FBI had told Johnson & Johnson that the tampering was local, and Johnson & Johnson could pull the Tylenol from just the Chicago retail shelves. But the company's leaders wanted to assure customers that they were doing everything possible to keep them safe.

What happened? Consumers didn't run away from the product. They respected Johnson & Johnson's decision. The company developed a protective seal, put Tylenol back on the shelves, and got five extra points in market share. Although no one could have predicted that, the company was resolute that honesty with customers pays off, and it did. Handsomely.

Intel learned this lesson the hard way. At first, they denied and played down the problems with its heralded Pentium microprocessor. Bad publicity inspired a quick reversal, and Intel explained exactly how the flaw would affect a personal computer's operation, which was minor. Intel then still offered to take back any computer and replace the chip for free. Was Intel deluged? No. Though the information is guarded by the company, most analysts have surmised that having fessed up to the chip's defect, Intel's number of returns was quite small. Though the company made a big mistake in a highly competitive industry, Intel's CEO Andy Grove remained a hero.

Honesty will pay similar dividends with suppliers. The key to good relations with outsiders, however, is to start within your own firm. It's very tough to be honest and open externally if you aren't honest and open internally. If you learn deceit inside, learn what to hide and how to couch things, you will go outside and couch things.

Toolbox for Speaking the Truth

Being honest and open is a habit you can get into only by repeated and frequent practicing in different situations—learning to catch yourself when you're obfuscating situations or sugarcoating things rather than dealing with them directly. There are several steps you can take to foster an honest and open environment in your company, at both the individual and group level.

◆ Identify a situation in which you are not being candid. Write down the ways in which you are being indirect or not stating all the facts. Also write down what it is you would say if you were totally candid. Then find an insider or outsider with whom you can role-play. Try out the new behavior—for practice and to experience what the likely reactions may be. Larger companies can set up training exercises like this with pairs of people who do not know each other.

◆ Apply the mirror test: Think about how you would like to be treated in a certain situation, and treat others in that way.

◆ If someone complains to you about someone else in the organization or about a business situation in the organization, ask, "Why are you telling me this? If you have a problem with Mr. X, talk to Mr. X. If you think situation Y is a problem, talk to the people who control situation Y."

◆ If groups of people are not speaking the truth to each other, interview various people in each group, then

---

write up a vignette that captures the implied sentiments. Give it to everyone in the group. Ask them to comment on whether the vignette is realistic, why it is occurring, and what can be done about it.

◆ Never hold a meeting unless a clear agenda, clear time frame, and clear objective have been stated. Also, review who really needs to be there; let everyone else stay at their work.

◆ Force meetings to be short. People will feel pressure to state their positions directly, for fear of missing their chance to speak.

◆ Never hold a "pre-meeting" to script what will happen at an upcoming real meeting. Scripting a meeting automatically closes discussion.

◆ Clearly list the information you expect from employees. Discourage them from working extra hours to generate other information that you don't need anyway.

◆ Always report the final results of a project team's work. Over and over, I hear managers complain that they worked on a task group for months and never found out what was being done with the results of their effort.

◆ Be polite but direct in correcting employees. It's more damaging to misguide employees by being soft than it is to hurt their feelings with criticism.

◆ Don't wait for a "reduction in force" to get rid of a person. Confront their performance problems head-on.

There are many benefits to speaking the truth. David Nadler, a consultant, likes to make an analogy to the Canadian moose. The animals weigh about 800 pounds and are smelly, and ugly as sin. They are easy to identify, and hard to ignore. There are numerous 800-pound moose in any organization, yet most people refuse to acknowledge them. The best organizations call a moose a moose, deal with it openly, and get it out of there before it causes more problems.

Just tell people what's going on. It's like Joan Rivers's opener: "Can we talk?" It's hard to name a company that does this all the time. But the degree to which your company speaks openly can significantly affect its fate. Historically, IBM was the prototypical company where everybody was "nice" to each other. But over time this false "respect" for the individual prevented the straightforward handling of important difficulties. PepsiCo, in contrast, built a culture around attacking issues. The result is a company composed of people who can confront and resolve business problems without being sidetracked.

Once you've mastered straight talk in your company, you will be able to tackle the next principle: *Inspire Concretely.*

Bringing Up Bad News

A fictitious vignette can spark discussion among managers and employees about speaking the truth. Here's one I use in the financial services industry. I first hand out "The Case" as follows. The people discuss what they think should be done. After they've proposed solutions, I present some recommendations.

THE CASE

After being at the Wakefield Brothers investment firm for about six months, Laura felt increasingly confident that she had a good sense of the preferences of several key clients. Among them was Coastal Investment Holdings. In the early summer of 1991, Laura received a phone call from Wakefield's derivatives desk in New York. Could she sell an "inverse floater" to the Coastal account? "I don't even have to ask them," Laura replied. "That is far too volatile for their portfolio. They never touch the stuff."

Laura developed the account over the next three months. Then one day in September her contact at Coastal shared with her that the firm had bought four inverse floaters back in June from another broker. No one else at Wakefield knew, but Laura feared the word would get out sooner or later. The fees were probably several million dollars on this particular investment. It was a big deal. What should Laura tell her boss—if anything?

DISCUSSION

At first I lead a discussion during which we talk about the various options Laura has. Managers and employees articulate their thoughts on how to best handle the situation in light of the principle, *Speak the Truth.*

RECOMMENDATIONS

It would not be dishonest to say nothing. But it wouldn't be very open, either. Of course, the right choice is to raise the issue, so Laura and her boss can figure out why the mistake was made, so Laura will do better next time, and so other brokers won't fall into the same trap.

What Laura actually *does* may differ from what she *should* do. It depends on the atmosphere management has set. If Laura has gotten vibrations that a broker's job is on the line if superiors find out they blew a deal, then she probably won't bring it up. But if it's been made clear that management would prefer to hear about mistakes so they can figure out what went wrong, then she probably will speak up. Management should favor this atmosphere over the oppressive one because more information will surface about what's really happening at the firm. Managers will have a chance to coach Laura so she won't make a similar mistake again. And they'll know that if Laura continues to make mistakes every month or so, the company might not be the place for her.

By the way, there is a secondary communication lesson in this story. In an earlier discussion, Coastal's portfolio manager must have told Laura the kinds of securities he wanted. She assumed the new issue was too volatile, based on that conversation. But perhaps that portfolio manager wasn't being clear. Laura could have run the opportunity past him. Obviously the security wasn't too volatile because he actually bought it elsewhere. Even after the deed was done, Laura could still benefit by bringing the matter up directly with the client: "I thought you weren't interested in this kind of security. Did I mishear you? Did you have a change of policy?" Chances are that then they would have an informative, productive, and honest conversation.

CHAPTER

4

Principle Four

INSPIRE CONCRETELY

How to clarify your company's values, the purpose of your employees' work, and the mission you are all trying to achieve.

When Robert Eaton succeeded Lee Iaccoca as CEO of Chrysler Corporation in 1992, he went through the challenging exercise of trying to define the carmaker's purpose. Eaton was an outsider, coming from General Motors, so he spent his first three months just talking with people in the company. He perceived that even though the company had good managers, an enviable product line, and an impressive product development process, employees had no real vision of where the company was headed or what it stood for. They simply moved from "one crisis" to the next. They were uninspired.

Eaton brought in my firm to help his top 23 managers define the company's vision—its *Values*, its *Purpose*, and its *Mission*. We met every third week, each time for a half-day to two days. The conversations were long and heated. After about three months, the group agreed on its values and a statement of purpose: Chrysler aimed "to produce low-cost, high-quality automobiles and light trucks." I then asked each of the 23 executives to share our work with five or six of their most trusted direct reports and to get feedback on the values and purpose.

At the next session I put the statement up on the board in the front of the room and asked, "How did your people respond to it?" There was a long pause. Then one fellow raised his hand and said his people seemed to be excited about the values, but they just yawned at the statement of purpose. It was not inspirational. It didn't say a whole lot. Indeed, they felt that the stated purpose to make low-cost, high-quality automobiles was just a rephrasing of the strategy Iacocca had articulated. It reflected a standard manufacturer's mentality. The others chattered among themselves in agreement.

Then I asked, "Well, besides just criticizing, were your people able to come up with a concrete alternative?" He said, "Yes, as a matter of fact." He began to read a different statement, and I began to write it on the board: "Chrysler's purpose is to produce unique transportation vehicles that people will want to buy, enjoy owning, and then want to buy again." As he spoke, the room went silent. Suddenly people became animated, agreeing that this was why people were coming to work every day. It wasn't to make low-cost, high-quality vehicles, but to make unique vehicles that people would want to buy. And the people weren't just buying a product they would enjoy but an entire ownership process they would enjoy, which got to the whole area of relationships with dealers and service. The ultimate purpose, then, was to create a car and support system that would make people want to do business with Chrysler again.

Chrysler adopted this statement of purpose and has continually communicated it to its people ever since. In my view, this clear, direct, believable, and tangible statement has been one of the main reasons for the heightened involvement of employees in the Chrysler organization. The employees are turned on by it. Even today, if you hear Robert Eaton or President Robert Lutz being interviewed, you will hear them give this statement of purpose. Recently a CNN reporter asked Eaton about how Chrysler's market share would rise. He responded, "I don't really worry much about market share because I know that as long as we continue to develop unique transportation vehicles that people will want to buy, will enjoy owning, and will want to buy again, market share and profitability will take care of themselves." Recently, the Dodge Intrepid won Best Car of the Year. Chrysler also led the minivan craze with the two best-sellers Dodge Caravan and Plymouth Voyager.

Company vision statements have been around for years. Most CEOs, employees, and industry observers disregard them as little more than platitudes. The problem is they are vague, incomplete, or out of touch with the reality that exists at the company. But companies have to have vision or they will twist in the wind. If a company can't articulate its vision in a strong vision statement, then it doesn't have a strong vision. It's headed for trouble.

To inspire concretely, you have to articulate three things: *values*, or what your company stands for; *purpose*, or why employees are working for this company; and *mission*, or what the company is trying to achieve. The values inspire workers. The purpose gives them a sense of accomplishment. The mission provides a challenge.

Clear Vision

Before we examine each component, let's defuse the cynicism about vision and vision statements. Many people think all the time and energy spent developing a "vision" is a waste. It's not. Just look what it did for Chrysler. Chrysler is not an isolated case. Evidence is all around. Robert Wood Johnson, chairman of Johnson & Johnson for 25 years, shaped the company's philosophy and culture, and spoke and wrote regularly on the importance of vision to his firm. James Burke, chairman and CEO from 1976 to 1989, and now Ralph Larsen, picked up right where "the General" left off. Johnson & Johnson is one of the longest running success stories in American business history. In a survey conducted by Ernst & Young in December 1995, 59 percent of Fortune 1000 employees said one of the best (and cheapest) ways to motivate employees is to show them how their work helps the company make money. Translation: Inspire them concretely. Give them a purpose, show them the results, and they work like crazy. "Employees who really understand generate much greater value," said U.S. Labor Secretary Robert Reich, a co-sponsor of the survey.

Of all the concepts in this book, vision best signifies how convoluted a straightforward concept can become. The notion of organizational vision has been around for decades, and it has been an extremely hot topic during the past five or six years. Still, very few organizations are getting it right.

For some time I have used a well-known Harvard Business School case study to teach companies how to inspire concretely. Inevitably, the participants are extremely enthusiastic about Johnson & Johnson's vision statement, which they call a credo. But when I turn the conversation to the visions at their own companies, they snicker and sneer. Not exactly the shy type, I abruptly ask the participants why they are acting so cynically. Someone always says, "Yes, we did receive a vision statement, but I threw mine out." The rest of them laugh because they've done the same. A *Dilbert* cartoon shows the firm's employees grumbling about vision statements coming down from on high. The punch line is that Dilbert and his cohorts can't believe this drivel is what the company pays senior managers to do. They're amazed this is where the big bucks are going.

I ask the participants why they threw their statements out. They say, "Well, it was just a bunch of highfalutin bull." I push further: "Isn't the Johnson & Johnson vision also pretty highbrow?" They say, "Yes, but their management really believes in it and follows through."

Aha! You see, there *is* great enthusiasm for the concept. There is just a lot of cynicism that has resulted from the faulty process of putting the concept into practice. You can't just hand out a vision statement and tell people to memorize it.

In my experience, perhaps one in every four companies is really deriving value from the vision they have articulated and communicated. The nice thing about this, of course, is that it has allowed me to compare the effective ones with the ineffective ones.

The typical reason that is given to explain why certain visions inspire and others do not is that the good ones have the support of top management. While there is some truth to that, the explanation is too simplistic and incomplete. Most often a vision fails because no one in the company has studied what the elements of a good vision are. There is a new collection of corporate visions (*Say It and Live It: 50 Corporate Mission Statements That Hit the Mark*, edited by Patricia Jones and Larry Kahaner). If you read it, you will see that it is really hard to find the common denominator.

Most visions fail due to a number of shortcomings: They don't include all three elements (values, purpose, and mission). They aren't concrete. They don't inspire. They are not communicated well. They aren't debated. They aren't lived.

I think the cynicism arises most often when a vision state-ment is incomplete or unrealistic. Often the statement presents some lofty, vague ideal like the "pursuit of excel-lence" without tying it to what employees actually do every day. Or it doesn't reflect the company's reality. All this talk about "valuing our people" isn't going to motivate anyone in an organization rife with hidden political agendas.

So what are the components of a strong vision? Let me draw on insights presented by James Collins and Jerry Porras. They received a lot of attention for their book *Built to Last*, but what I found really useful was an article they wrote in the Fall 1991 *California Management Review* before the book came out. Although the article was not mentioned in the book, "Organizational Visions and Visionary Organizations" present-ed a key point: A fully articulated vision has both an intangible, inspirational element and a tangible, concrete element.

The inspirational component is what Collins and Porras call the guiding philosophy of a company: a view of the com-pany from 35,000 feet. In contrast, the concrete component is a ground-level perspective. Many companies have experi-enced difficulty articulating a good vision because they are missing one of the two components. If a vision statement articulates only platitudes and philosophy, it's not much of a guide for people who are trying to figure out what they're actually supposed to do. They'll say, "Okay, good vision, good values, but what will we be trying to accomplish next year?"

In my experience, this is the flaw with about 80 percent of the visions that don't work. A vision that just flies around at 35,000 feet and lacks concreteness eventually dies of its own weight. Some companies say, "Our overriding objective is to maximize shareholder value." That could be the goal of most companies. It doesn't translate into tangible objectives.

The leaders of R. R. Donnelley, the world's largest com-

mercial printer, realized the need for this translation some-
what by accident. They had done a lot of good work on their
values and purpose, but it just wasn't touching people.
Almost as an afterthought, they added that as a $6 billion
company, they wanted to be a $10 billion company by the year
2000. That goal fired up Donnelley employees, who adopted
it as their own.

In 20 percent of the cases, the opposite happens. The
vision represents some very specific, tangible objective, but it
doesn't address what the company stands for. In these cases
the vision quickly becomes submerged in the annual budget,
part of the planning agenda, and the process for generating
products and profits. If all you have is a tangible goal for earnings per share or market share, and if there is nothing about
an overall purpose you are trying to achieve, the vision wears
thin. People will burn out on it because it focuses only on performance. It reduces the company to a purely economic
enterprise without any human face.

An effort throughout your company to identify your
vision—your values, purpose, and mission—can be a power-
fully constructive exercise. Yes, in the end you should
probably print and distribute a vision statement. The important thing, though, is not what the statement is called or how
it looks. What's important is that the elements of vision are
openly discussed, debated, bought into, and reflected in people's behavior from the top down.

A fully articulated vision includes a statement of values, a
statement of purpose, and a specific mission. These three elements collectively answer the questions: What do we stand
for? Why are we here? What are we trying to achieve?

Unless all three of these questions are answered concretely, the vision statement will be ineffective. On the other hand,
when the vision statement does answer these questions

straightforwardly, the vision can become a powerful tool that directs the organization toward a common goal and motivates everyone to rally around the effort to achieve that goal.

Values: What Does Your Company Stand For?

Values inform those principles and beliefs that are intended to guide behavior of all members of the organization. To inspire in a concrete way, however, the values have to be rooted in the reality of how the business and its leaders actually behave. You can't espouse a value of openness when everyone knows that secrecy is the chief operating principle of the company.

In any company, of course, there will be occasional inconsistencies between actions and values. Values represent the aspirations for behavior, and given our human weaknesses, we cannot always live up to our highest principles. It is the striving for those principles that matters. A visitor should be able to walk in and infer what the company's values are by observing how the people act.

It is also important to recognize that values have to remain in sync with the company as it moves along. They are never static. A dramatic example of the power values have, and how they must change to retain their power, is illustrated by events at Eli Lilly and Company.

Lilly's statement of corporate values had hung on the walls for years when Randall Tobias took over in 1993. It said the company holds "honesty, ethical behavior, and exemplary moral character" in high regard. It talked about "integrity" and "excellence." Lilly's people were impeccably honest. Lilly employees would never break a Food & Drug Administration rule and would be appalled if there were a quality problem with a drug that resulted in injury to someone. They would pull the product immediately.

Over time, these values, as practiced, led to an extremely paternalistic organization of extremely nice people. It was a very nice place, a good place to work. Yet Lilly suffered from lackluster performance. One manager told me that the key to maintaining an atmosphere of honesty, respect, and morality was honest communication. But he acknowledged that when it came to looking people in the eye and telling them that you had trouble with their performance, or confronting someone in a meeting over a business issue, or killing a project, Lilly managers did not do it. It wasn't nice. One result was that performance reviews were not serving any purpose. And if the review process was soft, the company's performance would be too.

When Tobias arrived, the whole health care field was in turmoil. Lilly's weak performance left it vulnerable in the face of sweeping industry changes. That's why the company's board brought in an outsider. No stranger to change, Tobias had served as a vice chairman at AT&T and one of the main architects of AT&T's transformation from a government-regulated monopoly to a highly competitive, global telecommunications competitor. He was also no stranger to Lilly, having served on its board for seven years.

Tobias moved quickly to bring Lilly's expenses more in line with industry standards. More importantly, he shifted Lilly's strategy to focus exclusively on pharmaceuticals in five specific disease categories. Abandoning the medical devices business, he concentrated on these five areas. He then committed the company to becoming a global business in each area and identified the capabilities the company would have to invest in to succeed.

Within the first two years he also sought to revamp Lilly's values. However, he faced a dilemma. On the one hand, he could see that employees clearly understood Lilly's values and that the values created tremendous loyalty. On the other hand, he felt that as practiced, the values had led to uncompetitive behaviors, which could not be tolerated given current changes in the industry.

After some shrewd thinking, Tobias decided to keep the same core values but to elaborate each of them. He said the company's values were the right ones, but they had to be extended to address contemporary issues. Thus, "respect" was applied not only to managers and employees but toward suppliers, customers, shareholders, and members of the community. "Honesty" and "integrity" were extended beyond ethical behavior to include open, honest communication, a much more concrete concept. These shifts put everyone on notice that the days of nonconfrontation were over and that a new standard of behavior was established. The value of excellence, which had stood in an amorphous way for technical excellence, was extended to include excellence in everything the company did. Under these new guidelines, performance has vastly improved.

These changes, while subtle, signaled very different behaviors for Lilly. Tobias has gone to work communicating these values and making them a way of life at Lilly. My firm has written some of those useful vignette situations and discussed them with Lilly's top 2,000 managers.

We go over the vignettes and ask if they ring true. The people say, "Oh, yes." Then we examine whether their responses to the situations live up to the company's values. That sparks a dialogue about values. Tobias has also engaged the company's top managers in a process of consciously looking at Lilly's behaviors to insure they measure up to its new set of values.

Values are particularly difficult to establish in a highly diversified company. GE makes everything from jet engines to plastics. How can its divisions, which are so different, have the same purpose or mission? They can't. They have to set their own. But they can share certain beliefs and values.

This is tricky: Overuse of such words and phrases as "excellence" or "quality products" renders them meaningless.

What is not meaningless are words that describe employee behaviors, product standards, and pricing policies. Jack Welch was quite clever in figuring this out. He described values in terms of each division operating in a common fashion. Welch had to invent the values. The *Work-Out* concept brings together all levels of employees in town-meeting style to identify crucial issues, solve problems, and generally find faster, simpler ways of doing things. People are heard and *action* follows. Welch thinks of these values—creating an integrated diversity, sharing best practices among business areas, helping each other, asking questions, and listening—as the glue that holds all these disparate divisions together. He's also been smart about purpose and mission. While these are different for each division, there is nonetheless an overarching philosophy (or threat) that says—whatever the industry, GE wants to be No. 1 or No. 2. That is unifying while still leaving room for specific divisional details.

Purpose: Why Are We Working Here?

The second element of an organizational vision is more overlooked, yet in many ways it is the most powerful. This is the element of purpose. It answers the question, "Why are we all working here?" Companies that fail to inspire with a concrete purpose miss out on one of the major levers that can be used to motivate a workforce. Several examples, including an old proverb, illustrate this point.

A young boy was walking into town when he passes a quarry. He first sees a disgruntled man chipping away at a stone. The boy asks, "What are you doing?" The man replies, "I'm chipping away at this wall of stone, trying to get a rock out of it."

The boy walks on and sees a rather nondescript man. The boy asks, "What are you doing?" The man replies, "Chipping out a stone block that is going to be part of the foundation of a building."

Finally, the boy comes to a third man who is whistling happily as he chips away. The boy asks, "What are you doing?" The man replies, "I'm building a cathedral."

The leader's job is to give that sense of purpose, to help employees understand that they're building cathedrals, not just looking for pieces of rock. All too often, alas, CEOs fail to set this part of the vision.

Another example comes from the book *Being God's Partner* by Rabbi Jeffrey K. Salkin in which he recounts that when he was moving from one house to another, he was filled with trepidation when he saw the movers, a half-dozen big guys with tattoos on their arms. As the day progressed, however, he realized that the men were incredibly sensitive and good at what they did. They handled the furniture with care and showed understanding toward the kids and even the family dog. At the end of the day, after the truck was loaded, the rabbi offered each mover a beer, sat down with them, and struck up a conversation. He said to the crew supervisor, "This is the most extraordinary move I've ever gone through. Tell me about yourself." The man explained that he had been doing this for about 15 years, and during the first seven he had been quite miserable about spending his days carrying heavy furniture. Then he had an insight, almost a revelation, that he was interacting with people at one of the most vulnerable times in their lives. They faced uncertainty and apprehension about their changing life. One of the few things they had to cling to was their possessions. The typical moving crew would come in and treat those possessions carelessly, even destructively. He came to understand that his job and the job of his crew was to provide security and calm at a time when they were under tremendous anxiety from other forces.

Again, this man has purpose in his work. He knows why he is there. He knows what need he is trying to fill.

That last point is crucial. In determining "purpose," managers seek to answer the question "What is the human need that the organization is trying to fill?" Until that human need can be defined, it is very hard to get an involved workforce.

I have been fascinated in recent years watching companies try to improve the scores they get when they survey employees on the organization's internal climate. Even though all the data tells them that it really isn't working conditions or pay that has people disgruntled, managers typically will respond to low scores by improving the workplace or increasing compensation. It's my experience that the way to make quantum improvements in an organization's climate, to generate employee enthusiasm, is to help those people really understand what human need they are filling by doing what they do. If they feel their daily work is vital to real people, they are more likely to remain motivated.

AT&T managers regularly do climate surveys of their employees to test how happy they are. The results usually aren't so good. Why don't things improve? Because the managers tend to respond with typical human resources solutions: "Let's revise the pay scale or put in flex time or start a day care center or review benefits." These can be important, but they miss the point. There is something else going on.

If AT&T hopes to improve the climate, what it needs to do is give its people a sense of purpose. AT&T has mastered double-talk. I would venture to say AT&T will discover its people aren't happy because they feel they're in the dark all the time.

It also helps to give employees complete information about the company. Thus, they can see that their work is benefiting the firm. When executives hear this, they worry about revealing "too much." They question what exactly they should be open about: Should they open the books, report earnings per share, or discuss the stability of employees' jobs? My advice to them is simple: all these and more.

Information should be withheld only if it's insider information. Otherwise, an executive who says he can't share information with his employees because the competition might find out about the firm's strategy is really just trying to protect his own turf by keeping others out. The benefits derived when people know their effect on the bottom line, feel part of the team, and are treated like human beings on the inside are far too powerful to ignore. Without these things, employees get a sense of aimlessness and frustration. If they feel that's all they've been hired to do, that's all they'll do; you'll never get an ounce of extra work from them, or care, or inspiration.

Nike, Inc., in Beaverton, Oregon, is well known for its very involved and dedicated workforce. In a field that is highly competitive and subject to undocumented claims of product superiority, Nike has done a spectacular job of developing a sense throughout the company that the reason people come to work is to help promote the aerobic and orthopedic health of the company's customers. Employees know the reason they're there is to develop products that will make people more likely to exercise in a way that will not cause them injury. People at Nike have the same jobs that people in any other company have: Some are handling accounts receivable, others are working at the shipping dock, some work on assembly lines, and others are at desks. But just like the stonecutter who is building a cathedral and the mover who is helping a family cope, Nike's 7,800 employees are doing their job with the notion that they are contributing to the well being of their customers. They're not just performing a job that has to get done. Employees who understand this create greater value.

Mission: What Are We Trying to Achieve?

The final element to inspiring concretely is the mission of the company. It is here that the vision gets right down to ground level, because it tells everyone in a tangible way what they are trying to achieve. The mission represents the most important stretch goal of the organization, something that is specific, measurable, and time-bound.

There are all sorts of missions. When Wal-Mart was in its first stages, it had a series of sales missions including the size it wanted to become. Other companies want to obtain a certain market share by a certain date. Whatever the mission is, it serves as a rallying point for all the members of an organization. If well articulated, that objective can then be shared throughout the organization so that all employees can see how their jobs and their departments contribute to the achievement of the overall mission. It is also important to note that because missions are specific and time-bound, they do get achieved. Once achieved, you're ready to set a new mission.

Thinking of a mission as a stretch goal is helpful. Since 1982, I have been on the board of a privately held orthopedic company that makes equipment for repairing serious fractures to arms and legs. Five years ago we decided to get into the business of making these products for spine injuries—a much riskier and more complex endeavor. Furthermore, the market was dominated by an entrenched leader and other competitors. We decided on a specific mission: to be the No. 2 player within five years. That goal was large enough to inspire the company, yet specific enough to tell each department what to do. We had to design the products, figure out how to manufacture them, find the financial means, and set time-based sales targets.

Perhaps the most famous example of a mission statement that an entire organization can rally around is contained in the famous speech that President John F. Kennedy gave before a joint session of Congress in 1961. He said, "This nation should commit itself to achieving the goal, before this decade is out, of landing a man on the moon and returning him safely to earth."

That mission had a specific, measurable, and time-bound

goal. And it could be cascaded throughout the government's space organizations in the form of different programs—to develop the appropriate rockets, a lunar landing module, the safety systems to keep the astronauts alive, and more. All the parts of the organization had to work toward the same mission. Just so this was clear, Kennedy referred later to the need for the space establishment to meet the national goals of developing a lunar craft, better engines, and the Rover nuclear rocket.

Ironically, Kennedy's vision statement also had the critical flaw of being incomplete. Even though the space program had a great mission throughout the 1960s, once Neil Armstrong placed his big boot on the moon in 1969, NASA found itself lacking a purpose. Actually, it had no clear purpose even during that decade. Okay, we have to put a man on the moon, but for what purpose? Why are we doing this? The answer to this question was never resolved.

I have scrutinized Kennedy's entire address to Congress in which he stated his dramatic mission. During the other 10 minutes of this speech, he was all over the map as to whether this goal would enhance national defense, inspire scientists, or increase the inquisitiveness of the human mind. Or given that the Soviets were on the same course, it would upset our world view if the "bad guys" did it before we, the "good guys," could accomplish the goal. At the time, the Soviet Union had achieved more impressive space shots than the United States had. Kennedy did appeal to this sense of national pride and responsibility by saying, "If we are to win the battle now going on around the world between tyranny and freedom, it should be clear to us all, the impact this adventure will have on the minds of men everywhere who are attempting to make a determination on which road to take." Well, that is about as indirect a purpose as he could declare! And even if you read into it that this was being done to outshine the Communists, how does putting a man on the moon help democracy overcome communism? Perhaps Kennedy was only implying this notion and not saying it outright because he wasn't convinced that this notion alone was a good enough reason to spend billions of taxpayers' dollars.

It is interesting to note that since the moon mission was achieved, NASA has had a tough row to hoe. To this day, NASA and Congress have not been able to agree on a new mission, largely because they don't know what NASA's purpose is. As a society we have not been able to agree on that. There's no larger purpose—or values—in which to fit the next mission.

Although a company's values and purpose may not change very often, its mission does. At the orthopedic firm, our purpose is to develop the best line of spinal instruments and implants for surgical use. Our mission is to become No. 2 in the market. Once we do, our purpose will help us define a subsequent mission. Maybe that will be to become more profitable in the niche or to make a run at No. 1. In contrast, NASA's problem was that once the goal of getting a man to the moon was achieved, nobody knew what to do next. There was no purpose to guide future action, and now, almost 30 years later, we're still arguing about it.

The March of Dimes did a great job in changing missions. For years their mission was to eradicate polio. They did it. Are they out of business? No. They have this enviable fund-raising apparatus and name recognition. They couldn't just fold it up. So they quickly defined as their new mission the need to eradicate birth defects. They're applying their capabilities just as effectively in this new pursuit.

Toolbox for Establishing Vision

A strong vision can be expressed in a simple, direct set of statements. Arriving at those statements is not simple or direct, however. The process requires a number of action steps. In the beginning, the process is led by the most senior management group. Then other employees must take part in discussion, clarification, and modification. Managers must encourage elaboration and translation of the vision so that it is meaningful at the operating levels of the company. The basic steps are elaborated as follows.

◆ STEP 1: Begin with a straightforward, although time-consuming, series of discussions among the company's senior executives. Meet off-site for a day or two, every three or four weeks, over a six-month period or so. At these CEO-sponsored meetings, hash out the values that you want in place and formulate the company's purpose. Articulate a mission or the single most important stretch goal for the company. Last, determine how to make this abstract discussion as vivid as possible in terms of what the company will look like when the vision is achieved.

◆ STEP 2: Once a vision is developed, it is necessary to communicate it throughout the organization. Your best bet is to hold a series of one- or two-day workshops with a manageable number of employees, where the framework for and the assumptions behind the vision are explained and people are given an opportunity to question and challenge them. It will often be appropriate to modify the vision based on your employees' input.

◆ STEP 3: Ask each operating unit to answer three questions: What role do they play in contributing to the vision? What is it they have to do to make the vision a reality within their organization? To what degree do they need to establish subvisions or sub-missions to contribute to the overall goal?

♦ STEP 4: The steps I have described so far may involve the top 10 to 20 percent of your employment base. Next, communicate the vision all the way down to each employee. Do not use outside consul-tants for this step. It must be done by your managers themselves. They have to stand up and communi-cate the vision with as few slides as possible, in their own words, and with the greatest sincerity.

♦ STEP 5: Finally, after the vision has been communi-cated and people are working on the missions that support it, *live* the vision from the top down. Do executives and managers live up to the values, or just talk about them? Do people walk the talk?

It's common to invite an outsider or facilitator to keep the discussion on track and to ensure its honesty. Work in sub-groups is often required, as is a sharing of ideas until a reasonable product is developed. Remember that it took us about seven meetings over six months at Chrysler. At other companies in which we have gone through a similar process, it's taken up to ten meetings and as long as nine months.

It is very useful as the vision is articulated and written down, maybe a half to two-thirds of the way through, for members of senior management to share the statements on a selective basis with some of their direct reports. In a sense you run focus groups to get people's reactions so that the docu-ment is not produced in a vacuum. Often during that process, some key insights will arise from people another level down. Just as at Chrysler, when you test it on the people, chances are that's when you'll really hit the target—together.

Kennedy's mission to get a man to the moon and back by the end of the decade was broken down into sub-missions for different units of the space community. The people working on propulsion described an internal mission to develop by a specified date a rocket with so much thrust that it could accomplish the liftoff. Similarly those in charge of the astronauts' safety set about developing space suits with certain characteristics by a certain date, and so on. In this way, each unit could play its role in making the overall mission come true.

To test whether the values, purpose, and mission have been understood and accepted by each employee, send an outsider into an operating unit. Or at least send someone from one division into another division. Ask anyone in that part of the company what the vision is for the total company and what that unit is doing to help make it a reality. The answer will go a long way to telling you whether the vision has really been communicated.

Part of this process is weeding out those individuals who may not be serving the mission and the values. In one of GE's annual reports, Jack Welch dealt with this notion by presenting a matrix with four squares that could be used to evaluate people. Across the top were results: Did the person achieve them, yes or no? Down the side were values: Did the person live by them, yes or no? That leads to four categories.

Obviously, the people who live by the values and deliver the results have long, successful careers ahead of them. It's also pretty easy to figure out what to do with the people who don't get the values and don't deliver.

For those who live by the values but don't achieve results, Welch advises giving them challenging jobs. Maybe they had a bad year. You give them a chance as long as they don't make a habit of poor performance.

The most troublesome category is composed of the people who achieve results but don't live by the company's values. In the old days, organizations would tolerate these kinds of people. Welch is trying to transform GE into a place where it's not good enough to just produce financial results. Employees who don't strive for more than financial results won't be promoted or will be asked to leave the company. These kinds of actions are how you inspire concretely.

Creating Buy-In

The process of creating a vision can easily become complicated and obtuse. What I've tried to show here is that the path to a strong vision is a straightforward one. It may be difficult, but it is not complicated. It requires managers who are willing to do the hard work of developing a shared vision and who won't allow themselves to get jaded by their purpose or lost in vague discussions. Ensuring this attitude is up to the CEO.

After that, vision requires buy-in. People need vision because they need direction. It is the role of leaders to provide it, and it is important to understand that the communication and acceptance of the vision inspire employees much more than the piece of paper.

Sending out a memo won't inspire anybody. Jack Welch goes to every training session for managers at the company's Crotonville, New York, facility. He delivers a message about the company's vision and values. He had a helicopter pad built there so he could routinely fly in from headquarters in Connecticut. Now *that's* concrete!

Johnson & Johnson, which already had a great vision, went through an exquisite process of challenging its vision and creating buy-in to change it. Although the company's vision statement had been in existence for some 50 years, CEO Jim Burke discerned that the extent to which the vision was really acted on in the company was spotty. In a Harvard case study, he is quoted as saying: "People like my predecessor believed the credo with a passion, but the operating unit managers were not universally committed to it. There seemed to be a growing attitude that nobody had to do anything about it."

So over a period of two years, he and president Dave Clare went around to all the operating units of the company. They conducted two-day sessions with the managers in each unit and people randomly selected from throughout the unit. They put the credo forward and then said, "Look, we want you to tell us one of three things: Either that the statement we have is great and you can buy into it and live by it. Or that the statement needs to be modified so that you can really buy into it. Or that we are just wasting our time on this."

Most people gave them the second response. They got suggestions on how to improve the vision, and they changed it using the steps outlined above. When they were done, they had a meeting of 500 employees at the Waldorf-Astoria Hotel in New York City where they unveiled the revised credo and committed to it. They had these people roll it out through the organization. That credo is now not just something that's framed and hung on people's walls. It is something that they talk about and live by. The success of the buy-in is directly attributable to managers' willingness to have people challenge them and the vision statement itself.

Burke was a terrific role model for people seeking to behave in accordance with the company's values. So is Tobias. So is Welch. You can't teach employees to share a set of values. You have to inspire by concrete example. Too many executives don't understand how important this is. I was doing one of my three-day seminars on empowerment, requested by a Fortune 50 CEO for his company. At the end, the CEO said, "I'm glad we've gone through this. Intimidation is out. From this day forth, empowerment and individual responsibility are in. And that's an order." And then he pounded the table and shouted. Believe me, the irony of giving an order to be empowered was not lost on the audience.

Buy-in has to be rejuvenated, too. After Chrysler's 23 managers reached that final, insightful vision statement, they rolled it out in two-day sessions to the next 5,000 people in the company. In the process there was some further modification of the vision. The 23 managers ran every one of those sessions themselves. There were no outsiders. Subsequently the vision was rolled out by these 5,000 people to all employees in the organization. That's how you get buy-in—by communicating the company's values, purpose, and mission from one individual to the next. Chrysler, in my view, has become the premier automotive company in America. While it is far from perfect, the people in the company have a great understanding of what they are trying to achieve.

Inspiring concretely requires a commitment from senior management to develop vision. It requires the involvement of every employee, and it requires a lot of communication. The process of developing vision itself is straightforward, but sticking with it is difficult. If you can just stay focused on the simple steps, you will make it.

The values, purpose, and mission you establish will guide your people in their daily work. Now it is time to help them make the right decisions when performing that work. That's the goal of our next principle: *Challenge False Paradoxes.*

CHAPTER

5

Principle Five

CHALLENGE
FALSE PARADOXES

*How to shed "either/or" thinking
and practice "both/and" thinking.*

*How to achieve short-term and long-term performance,
high quality and low cost, customer service and profit.*

In 1981, I was teaching in several executive education programs
at General Electric's management development training
center in Crotonville, New York. A regular part of the program was
a special afternoon session where Jack Welch would hold
a high-spirited, candid question-and-answer session with the

participants. With GE for 20 years, Welch had been CEO for about a year and had earned the nickname Neutron Jack, a way to characterize the kinds of cuts he was making in staffing. The joke was that after he reviewed one of GE's businesses, the buildings would still be standing, but the people would be gone, much like the concept of the neutron bomb.

During the session one brave manager stood up and asked: "How do I explain to my people that things are so tight that we're letting many people go, and yet here in Crotonville we have just broken ground for a new residence home for executives in training that is going to cost $40 million?"

Sitting in the back of the room, I thought the manager did seem to be pointing out a contradiction. Welch didn't hesitate for a moment in his answer. To paraphrase, he said: "You're exactly right. We are cutting people, and we are building the new training facility. However, I don't see those as contradictions. We all need to understand the imperative of doing both things. On the one hand, we do need to streamline our organization. The excess people were baggage, and cutting them reduces cost, which enables us to compete more efficiently on a worldwide level. At the same time, we need to invest in the skills and capabilities of the people who remain here."

Then Welch directly congratulated the person for asking such a good question. He felt it was important for GE's employees to understand his response, and he asked all the managers to explain it to their people candidly and honestly.

I was extremely impressed with the rapidity of Welch's response and the clarity of his thinking. He was saying that an organization can do two seemingly contradictory things. Indeed, when you examine the issue more closely, you realize there is nothing contradictory at all. There is no reason you can't reduce excess expenses and also invest in the future of the business. Eureka! The challenge is to not see those goals as contradictory, but to pursue both at the same time.

This got me thinking about all the instances in which managers battle themselves over seemingly unanswerable contradictions. I began to work through each of the classic paradoxes in business to see which ones sounded unsolvable but actually could be resolved. I became more and more convinced that virtually every dilemma we have traditionally accepted as an *either/or* choice can be turned around by the best managers into a situation where both goals can be achieved.

Customer Service and Profit

My thinking ultimately crystallized in 1992, when we were helping Robert Eaton and his senior team develop Chrysler's vision. In particular, we were debating what the values of the Chrysler Corporation would be. The conversations were long and heated. Chrysler never really had a values statement, and the automotive industry—Chrysler in particular—was known for operating in a ruthless fashion rather than a value-driven fashion.

The discussion centered on the value of customer satisfaction. The senior managers felt that achieving high levels of customer satisfaction should drive behavior at Chrysler. However, they were very concerned about whether the company could really afford to deliver such service and still remain profitable. After all, warranty expenses do eat into profitability, and extra service means higher costs. The debate, which went on for several sessions, was finally resolved when president Bob Lutz made the following observation (again paraphrased): "You know, I've been listening to our dialogue over the last three meetings. I think we all have to realize that we have to be profitable *and* we have to satisfy our customers' needs. We have to do both of these. After all, by virtue of meeting all our customer requirements, we drive ourselves into being profitable. On the other hand, if we're unprofitable and go out of business, we won't be able to meet *any* of our customers' needs. As I think about it, what we need to do in this organization is avoid the *tyranny of or.*"

This phrase, the *tyranny of or,* was immediately picked up and has become a catchall concept at Chrysler.

The Pitfalls of Either/Or Thinking

The *tyranny of or* captures the idea that I want to stress for the remainder of this chapter. Simply put, the best companies and the best managers do not allow themselves to get trapped by paradoxes, most of which are false and exist only in their minds. The challenge is to avoid the pitfall of seeing situations as *either/or* choices and figure out how to turn them into *both/and* opportunities. This concept is a simple one, but managers often prefer to wallow in the pathos of seemingly contradictory ends.

Part of the reason for this is that dialectics are rooted deeply in Western thinking. People are good or evil; issues are as strictly delineated as night and day. Marx declared there is a contradiction between capital and labor, and many in the industrial world bought it for 150 years. We love dialectics because by being presented with choices, we can then make ourselves think we are really doing something when we resolve them one way or another.

This is a serious pitfall in management. Too often managers see their job as making trade-offs, as opposed to expanding the range of possibilities. That is the difference between a manager and a leader. A manager sees a set of circumstances as a trade-off; a leader sees possibilities. Welch noted that there is no paradox in laying off unnecessary people while training the ones who are necessary. Lutz observed that there is no inherent dilemma between providing exemplary customer service and turning a profit. Both leaders pointed out that these supposedly *either/or* trade-offs were just a result of conventional, hackneyed management thinking. Once you get used to *both/and* thinking, you will begin to see opportunities to achieve dual goals.

There are other false paradoxes that are common in many companies (see Table 1). Let's examine how a few of the most entrenched *either/or* paradoxes can be turned into *both/and* situations.

TABLE 1: FALSE PARADOXES

Short-term earnings vs. long-term investment
Low cost vs. differentiation
Mature market vs. growth
Global scale vs. local focus
Wall Street demands vs. correct business decisions
Customer service vs. profitability
Mass production vs. customization
High quality vs. low cost
Centralized efficiencies vs. decentralized responsiveness
Market share growth vs. profitability

Short-Term Versus Long-Term Performance

In many companies, managers are paralyzed by the pressures for short-term performance and long-term investment. They see the two imperatives as an almost irreconcilable contradiction. How can they meet quarterly earnings requirements while also finding sufficient resources to invest in the company? This is probably the most widely perceived paradox in business.

Let me state unequivocally that this paradox is simply false. Organizations and managers who take this supposed contradiction seriously are actually engaging in self-pity and shirking their most primary managerial responsibility. After all, what is it we expect a corporation and its managers to do? The answer: We expect them to be make money today and to invest for tomorrow. That is precisely what management is all about.

On a grander scale, these dual goals describe the role a corporation is supposed to play in a capitalistic society. We expect corporations to allocate resources and to be an essential planning authority—to produce today's profitability *and* tomorrow's profitability.

Even in the true financial sense, the contradiction between short-term and long-term performance is false. It is precisely by being more profitable that companies are able to accumulate the capital and debt capacity to invest in the long haul. The best managers are those who can achieve both goals. What good is a manager who can produce short-term results but leaves a business in long-term disarray? Conversely, what good is a manager who can plan for promising results sometime in the future but never deliver profitability today?

A good example of a company that accomplishes both goals due to an explicit mind-set of "Yes, we can do both, we plan according to that philosophy, and guess what, we achieve it" is the spinal implant company mentioned in the last chapter. I have been chairman of the board since it started. There was enormous pressure created by the question of whether we should go for profitability or for market share. I made it very clear that we were going to be profitable *and* build market share. Yes, this caused practical trade-offs—if you added another salesman or engineer, that meant more expense and less short-term profit—but the mind-set was that we were going to achieve both. Today, the company has reached the goal of becoming No. 2 in the industry, and it is also as profitable as the No. 1 company.

The old ITT company got caught in the pitfall of short-term versus long-term thinking. They were great on generating short-term profits, and eventually they hit the wall and couldn't produce anymore. Apple is in similar trouble. The company keeps focusing on its fantastic operating system, but this is a short-term view. If it doesn't also figure out a way to get long-term market reach, it is going to hang itself.

Scores of books and articles have been written about the supposed inherent conflict between providing short-term and long-term performance, whipping the matter up into a highly complicated paradox. Once again, however, we see that the issue is actually very simple. The solution doesn't require pages and pages of writing and analysis. It simply takes one sentence: A manager should produce excellent short-term results while investing in the long-term health of the business. I'm sure this is what you already struggle with today. And as you probably know, this directive is easy to say and hard to do—just as with the other principles in this book. The solution is indeed straightforward; figuring out how to accomplish it is the tough part.

High Quality Versus Low Cost

Whenever you find yourself feeling an *either/or* paradox, try to turn it into a *both/and* opportunity. That may require considerable invention on your part, but it needs to be done. A good example is the seeming contradiction between high quality and low cost. For many years business leaders believed that it was impossible to produce high-quality products without also incurring high cost. American managers, in particular, were willing to accept this trade-off as an unsolvable dilemma. Then, the Japanese came along.

Japanese managers who rose to positions of power in the decades following World War II were not hamstrung by American business's false dichotomies. In the late 1960s and early 1970s, they began to show the world that it was possible to produce high-quality products at low cost. In fact, their sustained successes showed that the *pursuit* of quality can often result in reduced costs. One leading example was the practice of producing products to the correct specifications the first time through, eliminating costly rework.

Nowhere was the impact of the Japanese approach greater than in the automotive field. In the late 1970s and early 1980s, the Japanese gained a substantial position in the small, inexpensive segment of the car market. Toyota and Nissan (originally Datsun) led the way. Initially, these cars appealed to American consumers because of their low price. But as people drove them, they found that not only had they gotten a bargain, they had gotten a high-quality vehicle. The Japanese models offered more convenient options, got better gas mileage, and, most important, required fewer repairs and less service throughout the ownership cycle.

The Big Three in Detroit began to suffer because their models were both more expensive and of lower quality. Instead of taking on their foreign rivals, they eventually withdrew from the compact car market and concentrated on the mid-range and high-end markets. But that strategy was fatally flawed because Detroit still believed the same false paradox—that the "really high-quality" cars (the bigger, fancier ones) certainly couldn't be made at low cost. Wrong again. By the mid-1980s the Japanese were able to extend the same principle to the luxury car market. Honda produced the Acura; Toyota produced the Lexus.

These automobiles were of the highest quality by any

standard and were considerably less expensive than the competition, namely the Cadillacs and Lincolns of the United States and the Mercedes, BMWs, and other nameplates of Europe. Furthermore, the Japanese used the both/and principle in their marketing, racheting up brand loyalty by saying, "You know the fine quality you've gotten in your inexpensive small car. Imagine the quality you'll get for less cost in our upscale cars." This debunked the marketing (and management!) myth that the production of a high-quality luxury car required great expense and therefore resulted in an incredibly high price. The Japanese succeeded by applying their creativity and time to doing the hard work of turning an *or* into an *and*.

Fast Decisions Versus Wise Decisions

We can extend the same principle to the realm of decision making. Some organizations that I've worked with see a trade-off between the speed of decision making and the quality of decision making. They seem to think that it's not possible to make a good decision without spending a lot of time analyzing and arguing, over and over, about pros and cons. They get caught up in "analysis paralysis," living in a quandary forever and never taking action for fear of making some kind of mistake. To them, there is an inherent contradiction between fast decisions and good decisions.

However, in other companies I've work with—the more successful ones—management has figured out how to make good decisions fast. Sure, they still do the analytic work, but by defining the amount of information they need, getting that information quickly, and having an organizational structure and decision-making process that support lean, focused analyses, they reach a decision point, make their choice, and get the solution implemented.

At Nucor, a very successful U.S. steel company, CEO

Kenneth Iverson is known for sitting at the deli across the street from the plant, drawing graphs on a napkin, and making decisions. He is able to manage this way because his research staff provides concise, insightful data and because he has honed his ability to see unique relationships in the same old industry numbers.

Mass Production Versus Customization

One of a company's most basic decisions is which product line strategy to follow. It has long been presumed that a company must choose whether to mass produce a limited range of products at low cost, or to custom build a wide variety of products at low volume and high cost. This *or* has been accepted for decades. Only recently, with new manufacturing technologies and computerized manufacturing techniques, have most managers even conceived that it might be possible to produce a range of inexpensive customized products at moderate volumes to boot.

Time to wake up. Some companies have been doing this for years, long before computerized manufacturing was invented. Some examples include Hewlett-Packard (custom instrumentation), Electronic Data Systems (custom computing outsourcing), and Charles Schwab (custom financial services).

The principle behind delivering mass production and customization may be best exemplified in the restaurant field. Compare your typical Chinese restaurant with a typical French restaurant. In any city you will find only a handful of French restaurants but scores of Chinese restaurants. Yet if you look at the menus, you'll find that the French restaurant has very limited offerings at very high prices. The Chinese restaurant menu, on the other hand, goes on for pages and pages, with numerous offerings at low prices. I don't think for a minute that the proprietors of Chinese restaurants do much *both/and* analysis, but sheer entrepreneurship and inventiveness created what is now popularly called mass customization long before the concept ever became popular.

If you accept the *tyranny of or*—that you must choose between mass production or customization, you will find yourself believing it. What I am proposing is that you put your energy into doing both.

There is a variation on this theme in international commerce. It is often presumed that to be a global company, you must choose between two models. You must either sell the same product around the world or customize your products for each local market. Sony markets the same Trinitron everywhere. But food distributors like Procter & Gamble package and advertise a single item very differently in each market. In international business circles this is usually described as a trade-off between operating in "a global fashion" across the world or in "a local fashion" around the world. There are problems with each approach: In the former you may not meet local tastes; in the latter you may not capture economies of scale. These are the trade-offs managers think they must choose between.

However, the best managers and companies have figured out how to do both. The pharmaceutical companies have done a good job on this. They develop a molecule using worldwide economies of scale, yet how they market their prescription drugs based on that molecule is always a local call—which branch of medicine they target, whether they sell to doctors or hospitals, and so on. Another leading practitioner of this *both/and* philosophy is Asea Brown Boveri, the Swedish and Swiss electrical components joint venture. Chairman Percy Barnevik has been adamant that the company will have a global presence and take advantage of global economies of scale yet still operate in ways that are consistent with the needs of each local market.

Interpersonal Paradoxes

The false paradoxes I have addressed so far all focus on business issues. But it is important to realize that there are personal dilemmas in the workplace, too. Managers believe, for instance, that they have to choose between being tough with people in terms of achieving objectives and providing a caring work environment. Another false paradox is their belief that either they must direct people or they must empower them.

Why? These *either/or* situations can be converted to *both/and* situations. If you show respect and speak the truth, you can be tough with people and still show concern for their families or sit down with them at the lunch table. You can direct people as to what objectives or problems to solve and still let them create their own approaches and solutions. Indeed, if you coach them on how to solve problems for themselves, you'll be empowering them.

As with the business issues, there are a number of interpersonal false paradoxes that are common in many companies (see Table 2). Turning these *ors* into *ands* requires thinking through the types of management behaviors that can provide both. Often, when you strive for both sides of these dilemmas, the dilemmas evaporate.

Both/And Strategy

I have illustrated some of the most prevailing paradoxes in which managers find themselves trapped. There are others. The principle in each case, however, remains the same. So does the prescription. The best companies and best managers do not allow themselves to be trapped by the *ors;* they allow themselves to believe in the possibilities of the *ands.* They then go about the hard work of converting those *ors* into *ands.*

TABLE 2: PERSONAL PARADOXES

Directing people vs. empowering people
Downsizing the workforce vs. developing the workforce
Being disciplined vs. being innovative
Being demanding of people vs. being close to people
Taking risks vs. avoiding mistakes
Trusting people vs. maintaining controls
Knowing the details vs. delegating responsibility
Fast decision process vs. correct decisions
Respect for the individual vs. criticism
Achieving career success vs. achieving personal and family success

Interestingly, some of the most popular business strategists have succumbed to the *tyranny of or*. And they have been responsible for training almost two generations of strategic planners to believe that *or* is an inescapable reality.

For example, Michael Porter, who has made fantastic contributions to discussions of business strategy and to the analysis of industries, contends that a winning company strategy has to include a choice between being a low-cost producer or a differentiated producer. He argues vigorously that doing both is virtually impossible and dissipates resources. However, my experience says the best companies figure out how to differentiate themselves through either the virtue of product quality or customer service while operating at the lowest possible cost.

More recently Michael Treacy and Fred Wiersema have argued that to win in the marketplace, a company has to make a decision among three models: being a price-based competitor, a product-innovation-based competitor, or a customer-satisfaction-based competitor. Why must a company be limited to only one of these fine qualities? Why can't it produce the best products with the best customer relations at the best possible prices?

The mistake that is made in these kinds of analyses stems from examining companies at isolated increments of time. In any one economic period, a particular company may be winning in its marketplace because it has one of these sources of competitive advantage. However, marketplaces change over time. To survive, or, better yet, to prosper, a company needs both of Porter's and all three of Treacy and Wiersema's strategic imperatives.

Try this exercise. Pick up old copies of Wallingford Business Books, which provide examples of currently successful companies that have chosen one particular strategy. Find a book from five or ten years ago, and you will discover that their examples no longer fit. Most of the successful companies have either changed their strategies by now or gone out of business. Over time the marketplace is going to demand that you practice each of the precious few winning strategies if you wish to remain successful. This very simple idea needs to be embraced by more managers so they can get on with the hard work of achieving more than one winning outcome at a time.

Toolbox for Discarding False Paradoxes

If you accept the concept that you can manage your way out of *either/or* paradoxes and into *both/and* opportunities, then what do you do about it? As I give the list of tools, let me say that perhaps of all the principles in this book, practicing this one probably requires the most creativity.

◆ First, identify the major paradoxes that your company is struggling to manage. This can be done at any level in the organization. All it requires is an energetic manager to call a meeting of his group, in which he asks everyone to identify the major choices, the *or* situations, that they are grappling with. These can range from major business issues at high levels in the company, such as short-term versus long-term earnings, to basic operating issues such as driving a manufacturing plant for more output versus leaving sufficient time for maintaining equipment in top working order.

◆ Second, engage the group in finding ways to turn the *ors* into *ands*. All I can say is that managers have to focus their people on the problem and not let it drop until they find solutions.

I don't advocate waiting for a special event to start this process, but if necessary, the annual budget exercise provides one opportunity to force the issue. Typically, each unit of the company proposes a series of goals it wants to accomplish. It then creates an expense budget that it believes will enable it to achieve those accomplishments over the course of the next year. The dilemma begins when senior management reviews the budgets and realizes that too much money is being spent to make earnings targets. Managers go back to the operating units and tell them that their budgets have to be cut by 5 or 6 percent or whatever the number may be.

This establishes the classic *or*. The division leaders ask themselves, "Do we cut expenses, *or* do we hang in there and fight for our budget so we can achieve what we have already spelled out?" Well, it doesn't have to be an *either/or* question. The solution to the supposed dilemma is to find ways to achieve all of the goals *and* spend the lower amounts of money. It is only by working that problem very hard, by identifying expenses that aren't contributing to the goals, by getting rid of practices and processes that are wasting time and resources, that you can create the *both/and* outcome. Don't assume that just because the budget "has to be cut," objectives automatically have to be dropped.

The final step in solving false paradoxes is to admit when you've been beaten . . . at least, for the moment. If you can honestly say that you have pushed hard to think creatively, and there is still no way to resolve the two sides of the paradox, then it is time to make an explicit choice, and to acknowledge what that choice is to the boss and the entire organization. A business unit simply may not have the resources to pursue all the opportunities it identifies; it may be impossible to cut more expenses without jeopardizing major programs. If a division—or the entire company—has four major product development programs and really can't afford to fund them all, then it makes more sense to pursue two or three of the programs very well than to try all four in a half-baked way.

Let me stress that this is a fall-back position and should not be accepted until the entire organization has exhausted its energy trying to resolve the paradox. Real companies do have resource constraints, and tough choices sometimes do have to be made. But don't give up. And don't wait until the next budget cycle to try again. Once you begin the process of trying to resolve paradoxes, you can progress throughout the year with an eye toward resolving more of them—eventually all of them—as time goes on.

Resolving false paradoxes requires creativity and determination among a company's senior people. Their success, in turn, will hinge largely on a CEO who can enlighten and encourage them. Giving managers this kind of direction and letting them know they will be trusted in their solutions are two of the primary elements of our last principle: *Lead*.

6

Principle Six

LEAD

*How to set direction, develop trust,
and produce winning results.*

Leadership isn't that complicated. And you don't have to be born with charisma and brilliance to be an effective leader.

Of the many human qualities I have discussed in this book, none has been more confused than leadership. In the past decade there have been dozens of books written on this topic, each presenting two or three supposedly insightful theories of leadership. All this writing does not seem to have produced much clarity about what leadership is and how to provide it.

I find this ironic because it is readily apparent whether an organization is well led. I can usually tell within a day of talking to the various managers in a department or company. One of the things I ask is, "What is the goal of the organization?" If I do not get a consistent answer, I know right away that leadership is lacking. If I hear reactions like "What goal?" I know that leadership is missing altogether.

Instead of spelling out exactly what good leadership is, the trendy books give us numerous stories about some of the most famous business leaders of our time, such as Jack Welch, Ross Perot, and Michael Eisner, along with a seemingly endless set of conclusions. First, a company needs lots of excellent leaders, not just one dynamic CEO. More generally, though, the problem with studying these larger-than-life characters is that most managers are never going to become a CEO, let alone the CEO of a Fortune 25 company, yet they still have to know how to lead.

Furthermore, such tales provide little practical advice. It is like telling someone who wants to learn to play the violin, "Here, watch how Itzhak Perlman does it." This may be inspiring, but the student needs concrete instruction. Likewise, the business or division or team leader needs techniques he can apply in his own job or situation.

The Three Pillars of Leadership

At any level of an organization, leadership requires three things: Setting a clear direction, developing the trust of your people, and producing winning results. These three capabilities apply equally to someone running a three-person department and someone running a global powerhouse. Let's take each of them in turn.

Every employee wants to know the direction in which his company or business unit or department is headed, so he knows what he is trying to achieve. Leaders can provide direction by involving employees in the decision-making process. Or they can manage by decree. I've seen it work each way. What doesn't work is punting on the issue. Without direction, there is no leadership.

The second pillar of good leadership is trust. Trust cannot be demanded. It must be earned. Leaders develop the trust of their people by demonstrating that the direction of the organization makes sense and that the supporting organizational moves will help achieve that direction. And as noted earlier, one of the most important requirements for generating trust is frequent, open, and honest communication.

Too many people confuse trust with high moral character. It is essential but not sufficient to have integrity; just behaving in this manner isn't enough. Generating trust requires openness and consistent action. Leaders develop trust when they are open with their employees about the situation they are facing and when they deliver on the actions and behaviors they articulate.

The third pillar of leadership, which is often overlooked but can't be emphasized enough, is finding ways to make your organization win. Leaders win by setting high standards of performance and demanding actions so their people achieve that performance. Some managers misinterpret this to mean they must be hard-nosed or short-term oriented. My experience is different. Winning is achieved by setting and meeting long-term financial goals and by praising the good work of employees. The idea is to set high standards, hold employees accountable to them, and reward employees for meeting them.

Seizing the Initiative

One of the reasons leadership has become so much more important in companies is that it's harder to "win" nowadays. In the 1970s, most markets were stable. Managers just had to keep the machine running smoothly. Today businesspeople say, "Nothing remains constant but change." In this kind of environment a big factor in "winning" is being proactive. Of course, companies have to react, and they must have flexibility so they are able to react. But they have to go beyond this posture; they need to seize the initiative. That means the leadership bar must be raised.

Jim McCann, CEO of 800-FLOWERS, provides a good example. The company is only 12 years old, but annual sales have topped $250 million. In the past, floral retailers depended on national campaigns by wire services such as FTD. McCann established his own service and created instant brand recognition by making the company's name double as its toll-free phone number. His managers then built the most high-tech order and fulfillment system in the industry. Ongoing improvements have enabled McCann to lower tele-ordering costs and keep retail prices steady for nine years.

Branching out, McCann recently formed a partnership with Sears. The department store will act as licensee for McCann's flowers and gift products. The companies will have access to each other's databases for cross-promotion, leading to greater call volume. McCann has also opened 150 co-owned or franchised retail stores nationwide, which ring up 25 percent of the company's sales. Always initiating change in his industry, McCann has aggressively pursued business on the Internet. In 1996, 10 percent of his business came from information services such as America Online and networks like the World Wide Web. The latest innovation—gift baskets containing candy, stuffed animals, and other treasures—already accounts for 5 percent of sales.

McCann is a winner because he initiates change. Without winning, no CEO or manager can claim to be a leader. However, the converse is also true. You might be able to produce results for awhile without setting direction or developing trust, but it won't last for long. McCann spends a good deal of time communicating his direction to his top managers, and he places responsibility and authority for the various channels of business firmly in their hands. I've never seen an organization that can continue to win without having a sense of direction and trust.

Like the other principles in this book, leadership is simple to explain but hard to put into practice. I do believe, however, that good leadership comes down to those three tasks: setting direction, generating trust, and providing winning results. All the other concepts out there—heroic leadership, transformational leadership, crisis leadership, the psychological background of leaders, whether you should be born first in your family, whether you should be tall or short—get in the way of what leadership really *is*.

In fact, if I look at, say, the top 50 people of a major company and they all seem to be similar in appearance—male, white, tall, and good looking—that immediately indicates to me that the company is looking more for leadership style than substance. The people who can provide direction, develop trust, and produce winning results come in all shapes, sizes, backgrounds, personalities, and styles. The diversity of the group with whom I have been involved in acquiring and managing five companies has always given me great inspiration and solace. An Irishman, a Lebanese Christian, a Jew, an Iranian, and an Armenian compose our group. Similarly, I have always been struck by the diversity at such companies as Citibank, Rubbermaid, and GE. Diversity exists at these companies because they are true meritocracies.

One Firm, Many Leaders

There is one other extremely important concept about leadership, and it, too, is widely misunderstood. While the CEO must be a leader, leadership must go beyond just the top guy. The best companies have many leaders running their various businesses, functional areas, and departments. Each of the people in these positions of responsibility should demonstrate the three pillars of leadership. They are not determining the corporation's strategy or organization or reward systems—which should be defined by the CEO or top few executives—but they are providing the local leadership that is needed so that each of their areas can contribute to the company's strategy and objectives on a day-to-day basis.

A dramatic example of this point is the Walt Disney Company, which floundered in the years after Walt Disney's death. It was revived when Michael Eisner was appointed CEO, but he didn't implement the revival. Disney has the deepest management team in the entertainment business. The greatest act of leadership Eisner has carried out is his relentless pursuit of the best possible people to run Disney's many businesses around the world.

The companies that have dozens or hundreds of leaders are the ones that will win in the future. They are the ones investors should concentrate on, too. Chrysler has one of the best teams of middle-management leaders anywhere; that means it is a very good company to bet on.

A company needs many leaders, in part, because—for larger firms at least—business has become incredibly complex. You're competing in multiple markets, many of them global. That requires you to understand what's going on in Japan, in Hong Kong, in Great Britain, in Hungary. Furthermore, a technological explosion is taking place in virtually every function of business. What are the chances that one person sitting in one place with one set of experiences is going to be in touch with reality in all these situations? The likelihood of an autocrat doing an effective job at the top of a big company is slim to none. It might still work in a single-market company or a start-up, but once a company reaches a certain size, it will self-destruct without more leaders.

Even if one person could make all the right decisions, he or she would represent such a bottleneck that the decisions would inevitably be too late. I'm on the board of a $250 million company where there's an autocrat who has an unbelievable feel for the business. I'd say that 90 to 95 percent of the time he will give a better answer than anyone else in the company. But the business is not working as well as it should because as markets change, the information he's basing his decisions on gets old, and the company is slow in acting because everything has to revolve around him.

There are numerous ways to train your managers to become leaders. One of the best ways to do this is to design your own internal leadership development program. That's what Roger Enrico did at PepsiCo in 1993.

At that time, PepsiCo CEO Wayne Calloway was becoming worried that the company's long record of double-digit growth would be in danger without energetic leaders who could continue to expand the business. But PepsiCo's division presidents didn't even spend all the money they budgeted annually for leadership development. Perhaps they were using the funds to improve their balance sheets, or perhaps they didn't have much they considered worthwhile to spend it on. Calloway drafted Paul Russell, Pepsi's director of executive development. He turned to Enrico, chairman of PepsiCo's rapidly growing Worldwide Foods division.

Enrico dictated an efficient, 50-page document as the basis for an executive leadership program. Only nine managers attend at a time. They take a five-day off-site seminar with Enrico, then for the next 90 days apply what they've learned in their divisions while doing their regular jobs. At the end, the managers share what they've learned in another three-day workshop.

PepsiCo's managers are turning into leaders through what is in essence a formal mentoring program for nine people at a time. The company's results certainly reflect its success.

Other companies take an active role in honing leadership. Many are finding that "action learning" is the best vehicle for providing real-time leadership training; the technique also results in some great solutions for actual company problems.

Citibank provides an example of how to implement action learning. One of the bank's top people assembles a group of six or seven seasoned managers (10 to 15 years' tenure). He gives them a month to solve an actual problem the corporation has, one that is important to the company and on the mind of CEO John Reed. The managers are trained at the beginning and coached throughout. At the end of this training period, they present their recommendations to Reed.

A similar approach is taken at Johnson & Johnson. Anywhere from 10 to 20 people are chosen to act as an executive committee to handle one major issue. Again, the activity is sponsored by one of Johnson & Johnson's top five executives.

These kinds of exercises (and opportunities) promote the learning of leadership. The issues the groups manage are immediately relevant to the company, and the people are accountable for their recommendations. It gives them high-level exposure and experience as well.

Toolbox for Leaders

Some academics and social scientists question the value of a leader. They view leadership as nothing more than a social construct that has only symbolic value. They have even done statistical studies to try to show that the person who leads a business doesn't affect its success very much. The thought is that businesses are like baseball teams, and it's not the manager who matters but the players.

Obviously I wholeheartedly disagree with this notion. I was at an academic meeting once where the speaker was espousing this theory. When he finished, a person in the audience rose and challenged the speaker with a poignant question. The man noted that the position of dean was currently open at the speaker's business school and that the speaker had made a point to get himself placed on the search committee for the new dean. Then he said, "If leadership doesn't matter, why do you care who the next dean will be at your business school?" The speaker said, "Just in case I'm wrong." The speaker's response was clever and very revealing. On some visceral level he knew, as we all know, that leadership does matter.

There are a number of actions you and your senior staff can take to instill leadership in your company. (You might also assess each other on the following points.)

- ◆ Communicate that all managers in the company are expected to behave as leaders.

- ◆ Dispel the notion that this means they must suddenly have great charisma or mind-boggling entrepreneurial, twenty-first-century visions. Make it clear that leadership consists of setting direction, developing trust, and achieving goals.

- ◆ Require that each manager clearly state to his or her people what the purpose of their group is and what their top three objectives are, both for the longer term and for the next year.

- ◆ Make sure that senior management communicates in a straightforward way to all the company managers the basic truths about the business, without hiding any important facts or factors. Then have the managers communicate the same information to their people, plus what it means for their unit, in a similarly open and honest way. This will ensure that everyone in each unit understands the situation they, and the company overall, are facing.

◆ Hold all managers accountable to achieving both their short-term and long-term objectives.

◆ Train managers in how to become leaders. Consider an internal program like the ones at PepsiCo, Citibank, and Johnson & Johnson.

◆ Develop a performance appraisal process that measures how well managers fulfill their leadership roles. Design a way to critique whether they have clearly communicated objectives, have the trust of their people, and are achieving their performance goals.

The oldest management adage around is: If you can't measure it, you can't manage it. I agree. But while it's easy to measure output on an assembly line or the sales revenue of a salesman, many companies struggle with how to measure whether a manager is effective.

Too often, the evaluation of a manager's leadership is subjective, even political. Harder, more objective data can be generated with "360-degree feedback," which was described in Chapter 3. With 360-degree feedback, you ask the people who report to a manager, his peers, and his supervisor(s) to fill out a performance evaluation. It asks a series of questions that include the following: Has the manager clearly communicated the objectives of the company and your division? Has he expressed it well enough that you have been able to integrate it into what you do every day? Do you believe he gives you the full story when issues are discussed? Can he be counted on to make good on what he says? Are you satisfied with his level of performance in the organization?

General Electric and Johnson & Johnson are two of the best examples of companies that have developed leaders throughout the organization. Both companies have succeeded because they have taken painstaking effort to train managers to become leaders. Both have established practices to quantify if managers are succeeding as leaders. They also run meritocracies; they reward excellence of performance, not looks or connections or political beliefs. And they use action learning to turn managers into leaders. If you start to take some of these steps, your leaders will arise, too.

Leadership is the last of my six principles of good management. The final chapter puts them all together.

7

DO IT RIGHT,
DO IT FAST,
DO IT EFFICIENTLY

*How to make the right decisions, make them sooner
than competitors do, and make them
using fewer resources.*

W hen all is said and done, good management and good
leadership mean one thing: You make the right decisions.
Business is a field of action. You have to decide what to do,
when best to do it, and how to do it. Then do it. For consistent
results, good managers and good leaders rely on a sound
company decision process.

For years I have maintained that there are three criteria for
judging any decision process. The first is: Does it produce the

right answers? If the answers aren't right, it doesn't matter what the process is. And often, managers with less elaborate tools come up with better answers.

Now let's assume that two competing decision processes both produce the right answers. Which is better? Answer: the one that comes to the right answer sooner. I would rather have the right answer tomorrow than a month from tomorrow. So the second criterion, therefore, is timeliness. Do it fast.

Finally, let's say there are two decision processes that produce the right answers and do so just as quickly. Which *now* is better? The one that uses the fewest resources. I would rather spend two months instead of six and a $500,000 consulting contract to come up with the same right, fast answer. The third criterion, therefore, is efficiency.

The entire game of business comes down to making decisions. And the best decision-making processes are the ones that produce the right answers, produce them quickly, and produce them with fewer resources.

Just think of some of business's most notable successes and failures. They inevitably come down to decisions that were right or wrong, fast or slow, inexpensive or expensive. Consider a few brief cases.

It's 1978 and research laboratories have produced small, inexpensive, though not very powerful computers. Do you go into personal computers (PCs) or stick with word processors? Accustomed to a line of successful business ventures, An Wang picked word processors, whereas IBM, Compaq, and Apple picked PCs. Wang was just plain wrong. His company had a leg up on all of the competitors because Wang word processors were storming the market, but An Wang failed to see the future and even refused to take action to test it.

It's 1995, and several software companies are perfecting "browsers" to help people navigate the World Wide Web. Do they go public or wait until they can make their programs even more robust? Netscape didn't wait, whereas Microsoft did. Netscape, begun by programmers, brought in Jim Clark, a sharp Silicon Valley business leader with experience in high-tech start-ups. He told Netscape's founders, "You guys are doing just the right thing. This is fantastic. But don't you realize that we have a time advantage here? If we don't get our product out and financing up, everyone is going to beat us to the big market. Unless we have first-mover advantage, we will remain a nobody. If we get out there 12 months ahead of Microsoft and we're really aggressive, we can get enough market share. Microsoft and other giants will get their share sooner or later, but if we're out first, we will remain a player."

It's 1989, and AutoZone has just opened its 500th store, only 10 years after its first retail auto parts store was opened. AutoZone expanded due to good, fast decisions. Profits remained healthy, in part because the company reduced the cost of decision making. Under its original interstore ordering system, it took store owners up to 20 hours a week to decide what parts they needed to restock. The company installed modern information technology and a satellite system to coordinate sales and inventory information for all stores and between all stores. It reduced the weekly restocking decision process to only two hours. This not only saved time but also saved the labor and inventory carrying costs associated with that time. Thus store owners could not only make good, fast decisions about restocking but could make them more efficiently.

The goal of management is to make the right decisions, make them fast, and make them efficiently. So we can use these three criteria to test whether my six management principles stand up to scrutiny. Let's judge each one.

GET REAL is all about making the right decisions. Getting real means assessing matters objectively, clearing through the hype and emotions and attitudes so you can base your actions on facts. When you get real, you obtain a clear view of your strength in the market, your quality, what your customers think of you, why your noncustomers don't do business with you, the potency and cost position of your competitors, the potential impact of emerging technologies, and your projections for your future products. If you can coolly assess these factors, you are on your way to making the right decisions.

GET MOVING is about making faster decisions. Right up front I said the key to getting moving is to study a problem only long enough to solve it, accept that mistakes will be made, avoid witch-hunts, and cure analysis paralysis.

SPEAK THE TRUTH maps to all three criteria. Remember my anecdote about the importance of a company's R&D division being able to tell management the truth about how long a development project will take? If R&D says six months, but it will really be two years, you can't possibly make the right decisions. Remember how fast Johnson & Johnson pulled Tylenol from the shelves? It came to that decision immediately because of its respect for the customer. Telling the truth outwardly as well as inwardly, and making the decision fast, actually helped Johnson & Johnson gain a greater market share. Remember how Jack Stack turned around Springfield Remanufacturing? He opened the company's books, and once his employees became educated, they were able to make good, fast decisions at ever decreasing costs.

INSPIRE CONCRETELY also contributes across the board. It has three components: values, which inspire workers; purpose, which gives them a sense of accomplishment; and mission, which provides a specific challenge. As a manager you can deliberately use these components to exact good, fast, inexpensive decisions. For example, you could establish a mission to research a new technology faster than competitors so you can decide earlier than they can which new products might be feasible. Or you could establish a mission to develop more realistic prototypes earlier in the design cycle, thereby decreasing expenses in deciding whether to ramp up to full production.

CHALLENGE FALSE PARADOXES is fundamental. In fact, you have to have this attitude if you hope to have a good decision-making process. The unimaginative manager will say, "Decisions can be made either correctly or quickly. You can't do both." But the ingenious manager says, "You can make decisions correctly and quickly. What's more, you can be fast and quick and do it with fewer resources."

LEADERSHIP requires the ability to set a clear direction, to develop the trust of your people, and to produce measurable success. Winning results come from good, fast, efficient decisions. A leader takes pride in making the right decisions and conveying that pride to managers so they also put a premium on good decision making. In today's complex business world, a company needs lots of leaders because no one person can make all the right decisions. Furthermore, if the organization depends on that rare superstar who is right 95 percent of the time, he or she will eventually become a bottleneck in the decision-making process. Contrary to what we might assume, spreading leadership to other managers is crucial to making decisions fast.

Successful management is not complicated. However, it is very hard to put into practice. That has been my theme throughout this book. To help you turn abstract discussion into practical management, I would point out some traps to avoid and specific actions you can take.

By far the most important trap to avoid is getting sidetracked by fads. There has been a plethora of new management ideas over the past decade and there will be more. Sure, you should brush up on them so you can engage in intelligent (and debunking!) conversation (and so you'll know what Dilbert is talking about). And sometimes the latest fad will contain the kernel of a good idea; in these cases, the goal is to see if you can apply that good idea to help you accomplish the six principles. For example, consider how the quality movement, or reengineering, or the fifth discipline, can help you Get Real, Get Moving, Speak the Truth, Inspire Concretely, Challenge False Paradoxes, or Lead. Just remember that these ideas are means to success, not ends in themselves. Other than keeping current and applying the kernel of truth to the six principles, I strongly recommend avoiding the management fads. Inevitably, one by one, each fad becomes discredited over time.

Instead, concentrate on the timeless aspects of management—the things that good managers and good leaders have been doing throughout human history, without modern "sloganeering." Spend your time studying markets, the economy, and new technology so that you can gain a better sense of the realities in your marketplaces. Read a lot of company histories and articles that dig into what other companies are actually doing and how they are actually managed and led. Learning from example is the best way to figure out how to implement correct, fast, and efficient decisions.

Many effective managers read books on psychology to better understand the people they are working with and themselves. Psychology can illuminate many aspects of being a good manager: being candid, standing up for principles, developing self-confidence, and increasing self-understanding. It also pinpoints the traits of poor managers, such as false bravado and the self-actualizing exertion of power.

Another trap to avoid is making the implementation of the principles in this book complicated. I ask you to take these principles and apply them in your company, concentrating on how best to apply them rather than embellishing, convoluting, aggrandizing, or merging these ideas with hosts of others to attain some ultimate formula.

A fourth trap to avoid is the tendency some companies have to form an "effectiveness department" to oversee how managers are implementing a particular managerial technique. These departments develop a life of their own and become their own bureaucracy. What is most disastrous is that they let managers off the hook by their very existence. Each manager has to own the responsibility for implementing the six principles of this book and for seeing that they are effectively infused throughout the organization. Departments of human resources and organizational effectiveness can play a role in bringing special expertise to the effort, but they will never take the place of the company's managers and leaders themselves in implementing the principles.

Finally, never assume that you and your business are going to live happily ever after. Marketplaces and organizations change. The need to remain vigilant is always present. There will never be a trendy guarantee that business will last forever. That's why it is so important to stick to the basics.

A corollary to this point is to focus attention on the marketplace as it really is, not as you wish it were, and on your company as it is, not as you wish it were. Put the 800-pound moose on the table and deal with it.

Implementing the six principles is hard work. It requires a tremendous amount of time. And that is precisely why it is such a pity when managers get sidetracked by superfluous activities that don't serve the fundamentals. I believe that superior performance results from unwavering commitment to these fundamental principles. Learning a set of fancier moves without the basics doesn't amount to much.

Ask yourself a question. Do you really believe that today's winning managers are doing anything very different from the legendary managers of the past, like Alfred Sloan at General Motors in the 1920s, or David Sarnoff at RCA in the 1950s, or Thomas Watson, Jr., at IBM in the 1960s? Sloan and Sarnoff and Watson didn't have any of the "wisdom" that has been presented in the past two decades, but they got the job done better than anyone else. They got real, got moving, spoke the truth, inspired concretely, challenged false paradoxes, and led their people. In their time and in ours, the six fundamental principles have remained constant. The legends of the past, and today's legends in the making, have succeeded by sticking to them. You will too.

■

Epilogue

A Final Note Before the Music Begins

After reading this book, you may be asking yourself, "OK, Richard, where do I begin? These principles sound great on paper, but just how do I put them into practice?"

Possibly the worst thing you can do is sit back and wait for a committee to form that will try to articulate company goals and determine just how much of the truth they are willing to share. Whatever your position in the organization, you owe it to yourself, your co-workers, and your boss to begin now to act on the issues that you face. You can bet that others are facing the same or similar problems.

In the seminars I conduct, I ask participants to begin thinking about how they can get real and talk straight. To help them over the initial hurdle, I provide a series of questions like those included in the following three implementation guides. The first is designed for individuals who want to assess their position in their organizations and what steps they can take to improve their productivity or benefit from opportunities they may have overlooked. The second guide focuses on the organization unit, whether it is a department, a team of workers, a business function, or a profit center. Readers who are interested primarily in enhancing their managerial skills might find it most useful to begin with this guide. Executives, on the other hand, would profit most from the third implementation guide, designated here as "Company," because it highlights issues of organization-wide leadership and direction. Although all three guides ask readers to examine many of the same questions, they do so through three different lenses—the individual, the organizational unit, and the company— which magnify some concerns as they diminish others.

Not everyone, of course, is in a position to turn around the entire organization tomorrow and challenge false paradoxes that are deeply embedded in the culture, but these questions, I hope, will start you thinking about how you can get moving within your own sphere of activity and how you can inspire others to follow your lead.

Implementation Guides

INDIVIDUAL

Get Real

PUT TRUTH ON THE TABLE, *acknowledge mistakes, surface problems, and see yourself and your industry clearly. You will gain if you do. You will lose if you don't.*

1. In your area of responsibility, identify two or three realities you have not faced up to. For example, are your sales weak? Do you have low productivity? Do you lack new customers and face increased competition?

    Issue 1: _____

    Issue 2: _____

    Issue 3: _____

2. In addition to the above, identify two or three additional realities that pertain to your position in the organization. For example, do you fear that the company will overlook you for a promotion? Does the company hold your unit to increasingly high standards for quotas and performance? Do you believe your boss is unduly distracted by trivial matters?

    Issue 4: _____

    Issue 5: _____

    Issue 6: _____

3. For each of these issues, how do you perceive the situation? What is the actual situation?

　　　　　　　　　　Your Perception of Reality　　　　*Actual Reality*

Issue 1: _____

Issue 2: _____

Issue 3: _____

Issue 4: _____

Issue 5: _____

Issue 6: _____

4. What would you do differently if you accepted the reality of each of these situations?

　　　　　　　　　　Actions　　　　　　　　　　*Impact of Actions*

Issue 1: _____

Issue 2: _____

Issue 3: _____

Issue 4: _____

Issue 5: _____

Issue 6: _____

Get Moving

STUDY *a problem only long enough to solve it, accept that mistakes will be made, avoid witch-hunts, and cure analysis paralysis.*

RECOGNIZE *that the risks of doing nothing are often greater than the risks of making mistakes.*

1. Within your area of responsibility, what needs or opportunities have you recognized as important but avoided acting on?

   Need/Opportunity 1: _____

   Need/Opportunity 2: _____

   Need/Opportunity 3: _____

2. For each of these needs and opportunities, why have you hesitated to move forward? For example, do you face more immediate demands? Do the issues require more analysis? Do you find the approval procedure frustrating and difficult? Does the buy-in process seem daunting?

   Why No Action?

   Need/Opportunity 1: _____

   Need/Opportunity 2: _____

   Need/Opportunity 3: _____

3. For each need or opportunity, identify several actions you could take to bring the issue to people's attention and achieve an immediate impact.

	Actions I Could Take	*When?*	*Impact this Action Would Have*
Need/Opportunity 1:			
Need/Opportunity 2:			
Need/Opportunity 3:			

Speak the Truth

TALK STRAIGHT *with employees and create an environment so that they talk straight to you. The truth, painful though it may be, is always more constructive than unclear, guarded, or dishonest behavior.*

---

1. Identify a subordinate in your organization who would improve performance and results for the company if he or she had your candid feedback.

   Subordinate's Name:

   What have I or the company said to this person?

   What do I or the company need to say?

   How can I be most effective in helping this person improve?

2. Identify a peer in your organization who could improve performance or results if he or she had your candid assessment.

   Peer's Name:

   What have I or the company said to this person?

   What do I need to say?

How can I be most effective in helping this person improve?

3. Answer the same questions for your boss.

   Boss's Name:

   What have I said?

   What do I need to say?

   How can I most effectively say it while adhering to the principle of speaking the truth?

Inspire Concretely

CLARIFY *your company's values, the purpose of your employees' work, and the mission you are all trying to achieve.*

---

1. Do you understand your company's values, purpose, and mission? If not, with whom should you talk to gain that understanding?

2. Do you understand how your company's values, purpose, and mission relate to your business or department? If not, who can help you gain that understanding?

3. What communication activities do you need to undertake so that the people who work for and with you understand your company's values, purpose, and mission?

4. What concrete actions can you take to make your company's values, purpose, and mission a reality in your organization?

Concrete Actions

Values: _____

Purpose: _____

Mission: _____

Challenge False Paradoxes

SHED "EITHER/OR" THINKING *and practice "both/and" thinking. Achieve short-term and long-term performance, high quality and low cost, customer service and profit.*

1. Identify five major paradoxes with which you are struggling. These paradoxes may pertain to individual or organizational relationships or to business situations.

Paradox 1: _____ **or** _____

Paradox 2: _____ **or** _____

Paradox 3: _____ **or** _____

Paradox 4: _____ **or** _____

Paradox 5: _____ **or** _____

2. Now rewrite each paradox as an "and" proposition.

Proposition 1: _____ **and** _____

Proposition 2: _____ **and** _____

Proposition 3: _____ **and** _____

Proposition 4: _____ **and** _____

Proposition 5: _____ **and** _____

3. For each proposition, what actions do you need to take to make the "and" a reality?

	Action	Expected Results
Proposition 1:	_____	_____
Proposition 2:	_____	_____
Proposition 3:	_____	_____
Proposition 4:	_____	_____
Proposition 5:	_____	_____

4. If you cannot resolve any of these paradoxes, what clear choices do you need to make so that you aren't always in an ambiguous situation?

Lead

SET DIRECTION, *develop trust, and produce winning results.*

1. Have you clearly communicated the goal of your organization? Write it down. Ask five people in your organization what they think the goal is. Is it the same as the one you articulated?

   My organization's goal:

   Perceptions of five other people:

   1. _____

   2. _____

   3. _____

   4. _____

   5. _____

What is the level of agreement or disagreement?

2. If the perceptions are different, what can you do to achieve goal congruence?

3. What personal goals have you established for your own performance? How far do you have to stretch to reach them? By what date are you holding yourself accountable to achieve the goals?

	Stretch Factor	*Target Date*
Personal Goal 1:		
Personal Goal 2:		
Personal Goal 3:		

Implementation Guides

ORGANIZATIONAL UNIT

In filling out this section, consider the work unit with which you feel the closest connections. This could be your department (e.g., accounts receivable, advertising, or production scheduling), your function (e.g., finance, marketing, or manufacturing), or your business unit/profit center. The following sections refer to any of these as your "organizational unit."

Get Real

1. Identify the three most important issues whose realities your organizational unit has avoided confronting.

   Issue 1: _____

   Issue 2: _____

   Issue 3: _____

2. For each of these issues, what is the current perception of reality?

   Issue 1: _____

   Issue 2: _____

   Issue 3: _____

3. For each of the issues, what do you believe is the reality?

   Issue 1: _____

   Issue 2: _____

   Issue 3: _____

4. Why do you think your organizational unit has difficulty perceiving these issues realistically?

   Issue 1: _____

   Issue 2: _____

   Issue 3: _____

5. What can you do to get your organizational unit to accept and deal with the reality of each issue?

   Issue 1: _____

   Issue 2: _____

   Issue 3: _____

Get Moving

1. Within your organizational unit, identify three major issues that require action but have received none:

   Issue 1: _____

   Issue 2: _____

   Issue 3: _____

2. Why has no one taken the initiative to act on these issues?

   Issue 1: _____

   Issue 2: _____

   Issue 3: _____

3. What can you do to assure that your organizational unit gets moving on each issue as soon as possible?

   Issue 1: _____

   Issue 2: _____

   Issue 3: _____

Speak the Truth

_____

1. Identify three issues for which your organizational unit is either not telling employees the full story or is not willing to speak honestly and openly.

   Issue 1: _____

   Issue 2: _____

   Issue 3: _____

2. What is the company's current position on each issue?

   Issue 1: _____

   Issue 2: _____

   Issue 3: _____

3. What do you think the company needs to say about each issue?

   Issue 1: _____

   Issue 2: _____

   Issue 3: _____

4. What can you do to assure that your organizational unit deals with each of these issues in an open and honest way?

   Issue 1: _____

   Issue 2: _____

   Issue 3: _____

Inspire Concretely

---

1. Do people in your organizational unit understand clearly the company's values, purpose, and mission? If they do not, what can you do to help improve the level of understanding?

VALUES: (Circle one) *Understood* *Not understood*

If not, what actions can you take?

PURPOSE: (Circle one) *Understood* *Not understood*

If not, what actions can you take?

MISSION: (Circle one) *Understood* *Not understood*

If not, what actions can you take?

2. Do people in your organizational unit understand what actions they need to take, what behaviors they can adopt to contribute to the company's values, purpose, and mission? If they do not, what can you do to help improve the level of their understanding and the appropriateness of their actions?

VALUES: (Circle one)   *Understood*   *Not understood*

If not, what actions can you take?

PURPOSE: (Circle one)   *Understood*   *Not understood*

If not, what actions can you take?

MISSION: (Circle one)   *Understood*   *Not understood*

If not, what actions can you take?

Challenge False Paradoxes

1. Identify five major paradoxes that your organizational unit is struggling with. These paradoxes may pertain to organizational or business situations.

   Paradox 1: _____ or _____

   Paradox 2: _____ or _____

   Paradox 3: _____ or _____

   Paradox 4: _____ or _____

   Paradox 5: _____ or _____

2. Now rewrite each paradox as an "and" proposition.

   Proposition 1: _____ and _____

   Proposition 2: _____ and _____

   Proposition 3: _____ and _____

   Proposition 4: _____ and _____

   Proposition 5: _____ and _____

3. For each proposition, what actions can your organizational unit take to make the "and" a reality?

	Action	*Expected Results*
Proposition 1:		
Proposition 2:		
Proposition 3:		
Proposition 4:		
Proposition 5:		

4. If your organizational unit cannot resolve any of the paradoxes, what choices do the people in your unit need to make so that the group does not remain in an ambiguous position?

Lead

1. Does everyone in your organizational unit understand its goals? If not, what must be done so they achieve that understanding?

2. Have the people within your unit set individual goals that are realistic and consistent with the unit's? If not, what must be done so they achieve this compatibility?

3. Is your organizational unit committed to be the best at what it does, either in relation to other units in your company or to similar units in other companies? If not, what must be done to develop that commitment to excellence and winning?

Implementation Guides

COMPANY

Get Real

1. What are the three most important issues whose realities your company is *not* willing to confront?

   Issue 1: _____

   Issue 2: _____

   Issue 3: _____

2. For each of these issues, what is the company's current perception of reality?

   Issue 1: _____

   Issue 2: _____

   Issue 3: _____

3. For each of the issues, what do you believe is the reality?

   Issue 1: _____

   Issue 2: _____

   Issue 3: _____

4. Why is your company having difficulty perceiving these issues in a realistic way?

   Issue 1: _____

   Issue 2: _____

   Issue 3: _____

5. What plan of action will enable your company to come to terms with the reality of each issue? What can you do to help your company act on this plan?

	Company Actions	*What I Will Do*

   Issue 1: _____

   Issue 2: _____

   Issue 3: _____

Get Moving

1. Within your company, identify three major issues that require action but that the company has not pursued.

   Issue 1: _____

   Issue 2: _____

   Issue 3: _____

2. For each issue, what additional analysis does the company need before it can act? When could the company realistically begin to act?

   Issue 1: _____

   Issue 2: _____

   Issue 3: _____

3. Which individuals have to take action on these issues?

   Issue 1: _____

   Issue 2: _____

   Issue 3: _____

4. What can you do to influence these individuals and to impress on them the need for action?

Issue 1: _____

Issue 2: _____

Issue 3: _____

Speak the Truth

1. Identify three areas in which your company is either not telling employees the full story or is obscuring the situation. For example, does the company share financial data about performance and prospects? Do you know its cost position? What is the likelihood of future layoffs and organizational changes?

    Area 1: _____

    Area 2: _____

    Area 3: _____

2. In each of these areas, what does the company now report?

    Area 1: _____

    Area 2: _____

    Area 3: _____

3. In each area, what should the company say? That is, what is the complete, candid story?

Area 1: _____

Area 2: _____

Area 3: _____

4. What can you do to assure that employees get the full story in each area?

Area 1: _____

Area 2: _____

Area 3: _____

Inspire Concretely

1. Write down your company's values, purpose, and mission (leave blank if you are unsure or don't know).

   Values: _____

   Purpose: _____

   Mission: _____

2. If you have left any of the above blank, who can explain them to you?

3. Has your company adequately communicated its values, purpose, and mission throughout the organization? If not, what should the company do to improve the communication?

4. Do your company's values, purpose, and mission drive behaviors and provide inspiration, or are they viewed as irrelevant? If the latter, what can the company do to improve the situation?

Challenge False Paradoxes

---

1. Identify the five major paradoxes that your company struggles with.

Paradox 1: _____ or _____

Paradox 2: _____ or _____

Paradox 3: _____ or _____

Paradox 4: _____ or _____

Paradox 5: _____ or _____

2. Now rewrite each paradox as an "and" proposition.

Proposition 1: _____ and _____

Proposition 2: _____ and _____

Proposition 3: _____ and _____

Proposition 4: _____ and _____

Proposition 5: _____ and _____

3. For each proposition, what actions must the company take to make the "and" a reality?

	Action	*Expected Results*
Proposition 1:		
Proposition 2:		
Proposition 3:		
Proposition 4:		
Proposition 5:		

4. If the company cannot resolve any of the paradoxes, what clear choices must it now make so that it does not continue to waffle in ambiguity and indecision?

Lead

1. Ask five different colleagues what the goal of your company is. Do you get similar or different answers?

   (Circle one)   *Similar*   *Different*

2. If the answers are "different," how do you explain the variation?

3. To whom do you need to talk to get clarity about your company's goal?

4. When the senior managers of your company address employee groups, do employees leave better informed and more inspired, or do they remain confused and cynical?

   (Circle one)   *Informed/Inspired*   *Confused/Cynical*

5. If your answer was "confused/cynical," how do you explain this reaction?

6. What do senior managers need to do to enhance their credibility in the company?

7. Does your company have clear and realistic targets that will make it the leader or a recognized winner in your industry?

8. Which standards does your company need to review and set higher? Does it have procedures in place for rewarding people who achieve them and for holding people accountable for not reaching them?

NOTES

NOTES

NOTES

FAD-FREE MANAGEMENT

NOTES

NOTES

Index

Knowledge is Power

This maxim best describes why Knowledge Exchange (KEX) is dedicated to helping business professionals achieve excellence through the development of programs and products specifically designed to give them a competitive edge.

KEX's divisions include strategic consulting services; executive education, conferences and seminars; and multimedia, book, and online publishing.

The company's publishing division produces books that demystify the Internet, general business, management, and finance as well as audiobooks, videos, and CD-ROMs. KEX books and audiobooks are distributed throughout North America by Warner Books, Inc.

KEX was founded in 1989 by President and CEO Lorraine Spurge. Formerly a senior vice president at Drexel Burnham Lambert (1983-1989), she raised more than $200 billion for companies including MCI Communications, Turner Broadcasting, Viacom, Barnes & Noble, Mattel, and Tele-Communications, Inc.

KEX Chairman of the Board, Kenin M. Spivak, is also Cofounder, President, and Co–CEO of Archon Communications, Inc. He has served as President of the Island World Group; Executive Vice President and COO of MGM/UA Communications Co.; and Vice President of Merrill Lynch Investment Banking. He is also an attorney and a film producer.

For more information about the company or its products, visit the KEX Web site at http://www.kex.com or write to: Knowledge Exchange LLC, Publicity Dept., 1299 Ocean Ave. Suite 250, Santa Monica, CA 90401.

The Accelerated Transition®

Fast Forward Through
Corporate Change

**MARK L. FELDMAN, Ph.D., and
MICHAEL F. SPRATT, Ph.D.**

An in-depth analysis of companies that have
gone through corporate change, with a concise out-
line of proven steps to insure a fast, efficient and
successful transition.

Hardcover/$22.95 (Can. $28.95)
ISBN 1-888232-28-5

Coming to bookstores in 1997

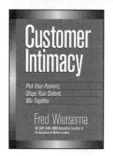

Customer Intimacy

Pick Your Partners, Shape Your
Culture, Win Together

FRED WIERSEMA

Taking business far beyond the concept of good
customer relations, bestselling author Fred Wiersema
presents a new way of defining customer relations,
which has produced exceptional sales, profits and
customer satisfaction.

Hardcover/$22.95 (Can. $27.95)
ISBN 1-888232-00-5
Audiobook/$14.00 (Can. $17.00)
ISBN 1-888232-01-3
Read by the author

Available in bookstores now

Changing Health Care

Creating Tomorrow's Winning
Health Enterprise Today

**KEN JENNINGS, Ph.D., KURT MILLER
and SHARYN MATERNA
of ANDERSEN CONSULTING**

An inside look at the health-care industry by a
team from the world's largest consulting firm,
laying out the essential strategies that companies
must follow to survive and thrive in the turbulent
health-care market of tomorrow.

Hardcover/$24.95 (Can. $29.95)
ISBN 1-888232-18-8

Coming to bookstores in 1997

Fad-Free Management

The Six Principles That Drive
Successful Companies and
Their Leaders

RICHARD HAMERMESH

A step-by-step program to implement the six
bedrock management principles that have a
proven track record in helping companies
achieve their goals.

Hardcover/$24.95 (Can. $29.95)
ISBN 1-888232-20-X

Available in bookstores now

Failure is Not an Option

A Profile of MCI

LORRAINE SPURGE

A case history that reads like a novel, this is the story of the tension, suspense, personalities and brilliant thinking that catapulted MCI from a start-up to a telecommunications powerhouse, forever altering the American business landscape.

Hardcover/$22.95 (Can. $27.95)
ISBN 1-888232-08-0

Coming to bookstores in 1997

Prescription for the Future

How the Technology Revolution Is Changing the Pulse of Global Health Care

GWENDOLYN B. MOORE, DAVID A. REY and JOHN D. ROLLINS of ANDERSEN CONSULTING

In a time of tremendous flux in the health-care industry, this book shows how those who can understand and harness changing technologies will be able to create the successful health-care organizations of the future.

Hardcover/$24.95 (Can. $29.95)
ISBN 1-888232-10-2
Audiobook/$12.00 (Can. $15.00)
ISBN 1-888232-11-0
Read by the authors

Available in bookstores now

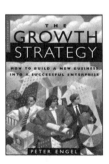

The Growth Strategy

How to Build a New Business into a Successful Enterprise

PETER ENGEL

A book that entrepreneurs have been waiting for, it shows businesses how to get beyond the start-up phase to become professionally managed businesses that will create true wealth for their owners.

Hardcover/$22.95 (Can. $28.95)
ISBN 1-888232-30-7

Coming to bookstores in 1997

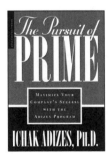

The Pursuit of Prime

Maximize Your Company's Success with the Adizes Program

ICHAK ADIZES, Ph.D.

The renowned author shows companies how to successfully navigate the various growth stages of a business and reach *prime*—the stage at which they are most healthy and profitable.

Hardcover/$24.95 (Can. $29.95)
ISBN 1-888232-22-6

Available in bookstores now

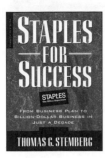

Staples for Success

From Business Plan to Billion-Dollar
Business in Just a Decade

THOMAS G. STEMBERG

Written by the man who made Staples a reality, this
is the gripping story of how a simple idea was
turned into a new, multibillion dollar industry (with
key lessons for those who want to do the same).

Hardcover/$22.95 (Can. $27.95)
ISBN 1-888232-24-2
Audiobook/$12.00 (Can. $15.00)
ISBN 1-888232-25-0
Read by actor Campbell Scott

Available in bookstores now

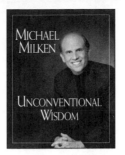

Unconventional Wisdom

MICHAEL MILKEN

The man the *Wall Street Journal* called "the most
important financial thinker of the century" shares
his global vision, insight and ideas for the next
millennium, providing a guidepost for the next wave
of successful businesses.

Hardcover/$25.00 (Can. $30.00)
ISBN 1-888232-12-9

Coming to bookstores in 1997

The Tao of Coaching

Motivate Your Employees
to Become All-Star Managers

MAX LANDSBERG

A must-read for anyone who wants to get the
most out of their *human capital*, this book presents
a new way of approaching people management that
will allow your managers to use their time better
while motivating, developing and creating loyalty
among employees.

Hardcover/$22.95 (Can. $28.95)
ISBN 1-888232-34-X

Coming to bookstores in 1997

The World On Time

The 11 Management Principles That
Made FedEx an Overnight Sensation

JAMES C. WETHERBE

Learn how Federal Express became a phenomenal
success and discover the eleven innovative
management strategies they employed, which
have set the standard for the way businesses
manage time and information, handle logistics
and serve customers.

Hardcover/$22.95 (Can. $27.95)
ISBN 1-888232-064
Audiobook/$12.00 (Can. $15.00)
ISBN 1-888232-07-2
Read by the author

Available in bookstores now

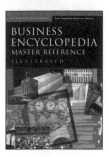

Business Encyclopedia: Master Reference

**KNOWLEDGE EXCHANGE
EDITORIAL BOARD**

The ultimate business tool and the ultimate business gift, this illustrated reference book provides a wealth of information and advice on eight critical disciplines: accounting, economics, finance, marketing, management, operations, strategy and technology.

Hardcover/$45.00 (Can. $54.00)
ISBN 1-888232-05-6

Available in bookstores now

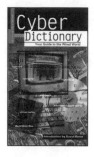

CyberDictionary

Your Guide to the Wired World

**EDITED AND INTRODUCED BY
DAVID MORSE**

In clear, concise language, CyberDictionary makes sense of the wide-open frontier of cyberspace with information useful to the novice and the cyber-pro alike.

Trade Paperback/$17.95 (Can. $21.95)
ISBN 1-888232-04-8

Available in bookstores now

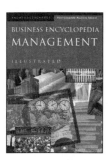

Business Encyclopedia: Management

**KNOWLEDGE EXCHANGE
EDITORIAL BOARD**

Volume two of the Business Encyclopedia series, this book is an essential management tool providing in-depth information on hundreds of key management terms, techniques and practices—and practical advice on how to apply them to your business.

Hardcover/$28.00 (Can. $34.95)
ISBN 1-888232-32-3

Coming to bookstores in 1997

60-Second Net Finder

**AFFINITY COMMUNICATIONS
AND KNOWLEDGE EXCHANGE
EDITORIAL BOARD**

For people who want information from the Internet and want it now, this book shows where to find anything you want, in sixty seconds or less.

Trade Paperback/$24.95 (Can. $29.95)
ISBN 1-888232-26-9

Coming to bookstores in 1997

Free Tote with Purchase of Three Books!*

I'd like to purchase the following books:

Number of copies

_____ **60-Second Net Finder**

_____ **Business Encyclopedia: Master Reference**

_____ **Customer Intimacy**
_____ Also available as an audiobook

_____ **CyberDictionary**

_____ **Fad-Free Management**

_____ **Prescription for the Future**
_____ Also available as an audiobook

_____ **Staples for Success**
_____ Also available as an audiobook

_____ **The Pursuit of Prime**

_____ **The World On Time**
_____ Also available as an audiobook

Name_____E-mail _____

Company_____Title_____

Address_____

City, State, Zip _____

Telephone _____Fax _____

Form of payment:
❑ Check (Make checks payable to **Knowledge Exchange, LLC**)   ❑ Credit card

Card #_____Exp. Date _____Card type _____

Cardholder's signature: _____

Tell us more about yourself:

Occupation	Where do you buy business books?	How many business books do you buy a year?	Age Group
❑ Professional			❑ 18–28
❑ Technical	❑ Bookstore	❑ 0–3	❑ 29–34
❑ Clerical	❑ Mail Order	❑ 4–10	❑ 35–45
❑ Other	❑ Warehouse Store	❑ 11–15	❑ 45–over
	❑ Other	❑ 16 or more	

Knowledge Exchange products are available wherever books are sold.
To order by fax, photocopy this page and fax to 714.261.6137
or call toll-free to order with your credit card

1.888.394.5996

*Offer expires Dec. 31, 1997 or while supplies last

Shipping and handling is $4.95 for the first book, $1 for each additional book, $2 additional for each _Business Encyclopedia_. Shipping is via Priority Mail. California residents please add 8.25% sales tax.